Clematis
& Climbers

THE ROYAL HORTICULTURAL SOCIETY

Clematis
& Climbers

David Gardner

LONDON, NEW YORK, MUNICH, MELBOURNE, DELHI

SENIOR EDITOR Zia Allaway
SENIOR DESIGNERS Rachael Smith,
Vanessa Hamilton
MANAGING EDITOR Anna Kruger
MANAGING ART EDITOR Alison Donovan
DTP DESIGNER Louise Waller
PICTURE RESEARCH Lucy Claxton,
Richard Dabb, Mel Watson
PRODUCTION CONTROLLER Rebecca Short

PRODUCED FOR DORLING KINDERSLEY
Airedale Publishing Limited
CREATIVE DIRECTOR Ruth Prentice
PRODUCTION MANAGER Amanda Jensen

PHOTOGRAPHY Mark Winwood

First published in Great Britain in 2007 by
Dorling Kindersley Ltd
Penguin Books Ltd
80 Strand
London WC2R 0RL

2 4 6 8 10 9 7 5 3

A CIP catalogue record for this book is available
from the British Library.

ISBN 9781405315913

Reproduced by Colourscan, Singapore
Printed and bound by Star Standard, Singapore

Discover more at
www.dk.com

Contents

Decorating with climbers

Climbing plants offer the gardener a wealth of exciting possibilities. You can wrap pergolas, arches, and arbours with scented flowers and lush foliage to create stunning features, or grow climbers in containers to add height to a patio display. Climbing plants threaded through trees or shrubs double the impact of both types of plant, while drab boundaries can be transformed into beautiful green and flowery screens. Even some of the most undesirable features in your garden will disappear under a veil of leafy stems. Flick through this chapter for these and many more inspirational ideas for climbing plants.

Climbers for pergolas, arches, and arbours

Provide an elegant structure for climbers to make their home and they will reward you with glorious displays of colour and scent. Whether you choose a contemporary pergola, a rustic arch, or a traditional rose arbour, there are climbers to transform each one into a feast for the eyes.

Pictures clockwise from top left

Pergola pillars The substantial supports of this wooden pergola have been masked with the sweet-scented blooms of star jasmine (*Trachelospermum jasminoides*). With a table and chairs positioned nearby, this setting is perfect for relaxing and admiring the garden. A climbing rose coupled with a clematis would make an equally attractive display. Try a different rose/clematis combination on each pillar for a multicoloured effect, and use plants that flower in each season to prolong the interest.

Framed pathway Paths that lead to a focal point within the garden can be enhanced by spanning the walkway with an arch and framing the focal point with a floral surround. Here, a wooden bench is accentuated by the cascade of climbing rose flowers that spill over the metal framework of a rose arch and cleverly entice the viewer to explore new areas of the garden. Experiment with other focal points, such as a statue, bird bath, or even a specimen tree or shrub, that will draw the eye.

Temporary arch A lightweight bamboo arch can be erected quickly and placed almost anywhere in the garden. Annual climbers, such as sweet peas (*Lathyrus odoratus*), will happily cling to it, providing a long-lasting, fragrant display in the summer. For a more contemporary look, bolt-together, lightweight metal arches can be used for a season, long enough for an annual-flower display. They can then be dismantled and stored until the following year.

Climbers for pergolas, arches, and arbours *continued*

Pictures from left to right

Framing a view A carefully positioned archway clad in ivy (*Hedera colchica*) creates a green frame as its ragged outline of foliage focuses attention on a display of red hot pokers (*Kniphofia*) in another part of the garden. Keep frames simple for the greatest impact.

Exotic bougainvillea The vibrant pink blooms of a bougainvillea snaking its way up a whitewashed pergola and the vermilion pelargoniums convey images of the Mediterranean. Along with the brightly coloured garden furniture, this scene is reminiscent of holidays spent in warmer climes. Bring the bougainvillea under cover in frost-prone areas.

Honeysuckle arbour For the ultimate sensory experience, drape an arbour with a heavenly scented honeysuckle (*Lonicera*). Imagine sitting here watching the bees while enjoying the sweet fragrance.

Clematis arch The rusting surface of this metal arch is the ideal support for the dazzling purple flowers of this clematis as it winds its way upwards, peeking through both sides of the framework.

Climbers for containers

Growing climbers need not be limited to borders and beds – containers of all shapes and sizes can provide interesting homes for them, too. From terracotta pots and wicker frames to hanging baskets and galvanized metal planters, the range of containers suitable for growing climbers is huge. As long as they have drainage holes, almost anything goes.

Pictures clockwise from top left
Tree decoration *Clematis* 'Silver Moon', with its silver-mauve flowers, completely engulfs this hanging basket, giving a 360° summer flower display.
Traditional wicker frame A vigorous climber is needed to make full use of this traditional frame. Here, a Spanish flag (*Ipomoea lobata*) threads itself through the frame, creating a spectacular show of yellow, orange, and red, firework-shaped blooms.
Ivy lollipops Wrapped around central supports, these two ivy (*Hedera*) plants have been formed into lollipops by careful training and clipping.
Topiary hearts Two small ivies (*Hedera*) have been trained over heart-shaped wire frames to create a simple but effective display. As the plants increase in size, regular clipping with a pair of secateurs will help to maintain their form.

Climbers for containers *continued*

Pictures clockwise from top left

Wooden pyramid Sitting neatly over a terracotta pot, this wooden pyramid provides interest as well as support for the dainty, rose-pink flowers of *Lophospermum erubescens*. It also adds height to a patio display. Turning the pot and pyramid occasionally, so that all sides are exposed to the sun, will ensure even growth. In time, the climber should cover the pyramid completely.

Single spiral In a square ceramic pot, a clematis grows up a single, spiral support, making a colourful pillar of summer blooms. If you plant four or five compact clematis in this way with a repeating pattern of pink and then purple, and group the pots together, you will have a simple but eye-catching design.

Awkward corners Climbers growing in containers are perfect for livening up dull walls and buildings. This evergreen star jasmine (*Trachelospermum jasminoides*) planted in a large terracotta pot has been set between timber walls, providing colour and scent as it climbs up the single, vertical support. The vivid blue wood provides the perfect backdrop for the pure white flowers.

Sweet pea tower A large, galvanized metal planter gives fragrant sweet peas (*Lathyrus odoratus*) the deep root run they need to help them sprint up a large, wicker tripod and smother it with blue and pink flowers. Masking the top edge of the planter are mounds of cascading orange and red nasturtiums (*Tropaeolum majus*).

Trailing climbers If they are given no support, some climbers make fantastic trailing plants in containers. This colourful windowbox has been filled with yellow and purple pansies (*Viola*), lobelia, and *Helichrysum*, while ivy (*Hedera*), planted as edging, creates a waterfall effect, cascading down over the front of the windowbox and almost concealing it from view.

Growing climbers through trees and shrubs

Living supports and dead tree trunks make some of the finest backdrops for climbing plants, so if you have trees and shrubs in your garden, try looking at them in a different light. Increase their worth by encouraging climbers to embrace their forms; experiment to see what combinations work well together to create a classy double act.

Pictures clockwise from left
Background bark Dead tree trunks with their gnarled, fissured bark are the perfect canvas to showcase the brilliant blue, trumpet blooms of morning glory (*Ipomoea tricolor* 'Heavenly Blue'). Plant them around the base of the trunk or in pots, and give them a head start with a few lengths of wire tacked to the tree trunk for support. Grow a combination of colours for a more vibrant show.
Autumn colour As autumn sets in, the leaves of vines (*Vitis*) turn a vivid red as they appear to hover above the green foliage of a dogwood (*Cornus*). Although this dramatic display is short-lived, it is bound to be a talking point, and adds an exciting finale to the garden performance before winter sets in.
Synchronized flowering Timing is everything as shown here by the clever combination of *Ceanothus arboreus* 'Trewithen Blue' and *Clematis montana* var. *rubens*. This striking show of flower form and colour occurs from late spring to early summer. Directing the stems of the clematis through the ceanothus, as necessary, will maximize the overall effect.
Double impact In the same vein, the star-like, pink blooms of *Clematis alpina* pepper the crown of a small apple tree, which is also in full flower with its little, dusky pink bouquets.

Climbers to clothe garden features

You can use climbers as living blankets of colour to add interest and drama to a range of garden features, from a dull trellis to a prized collection of terracotta flowerpots. For the most natural effect, allow the plants to climb and trail at will.

Pictures clockwise from left

Pot display This large storage rack, piled high with a collection of treasured terracotta flowerpots, has been draped with a blanket of *Clematis montana*. The wandering stems have successfully broken up the straight edges of the rack and help to underline the repeating pattern of the stacked pots. The pale pink flowers complement the terracotta, softening the whole display.

Statue companion A combination of hops (*Humulus lupulus*) and golden hops (*Humulus lupulus* 'Aureus') embrace this stone statue, while an exuberant patio rose provides interest at a lower level.

Trellis camouflage The soft green foliage and eye-catching flowers of clematis make them favourite climbers for breaking up the outline of trellis fencing. *Clematis florida* var. *sieboldiana* pokes out from both sides of this plain timber trellis, transforming it into an attractive garden feature.

Climbers to disguise eyesores

Camouflage unsightly features and areas of the garden with beautiful climbing plants. Whether you need temporary cover or a permanent living shield, there will always be a climber to suit your requirements.

Pictures clockwise from top left

Finishing touch Even the best-looking compost bins need help to transform them into decorative garden features. Surround them with supporting trellis for climbers, such as this lavender-flowered rose, to soften their appearance and distract the eye.

Autumn shroud This tiny shed is cloaked in the autumnal tints of *Vitis coignetiae* – its large, heart-shaped leaves turn from green to a fiery mix of blood-red and yellow as the temperature falls.

All-over cover This wooden shed has all but disappeared under a cloak of *Actinidia kolomikta* and white-flowered *Solanum laxum* 'Album'. Plant climbers on as many sides of a structure as you can to gain the maximum benefit from nature's camouflage.

Elegant disguise Obscure the outline of a water butt by training a swathe of clematis over and around it. The eye is instinctively drawn to the beautiful white flowers of *Clematis* 'Miss Bateman' rather than to the butt.

Adding height to a border

With their ability to break through the lower levels of border planting, climbers can create exciting focal points in a garden. They show their faces at, or above, head height and are invaluable additions to any display.

Pictures clockwise from left

Wooden obelisk A stately wooden obelisk bedecked with clusters of soft-pink blooms of a double-flowered climbing rose has to be a winning combination in anyone's books. Climbing roses are heavy plants, becoming increasingly so with age, and require supports of considerable strength to hold them up. Prune them regularly to maintain top-quality flowers.

Soaring colour A vivid pink clematis teamed with a deep blue California lilac (*Ceanothus*) creates a vertical palette of colour up a willow fence.

Border impact Where a border backs onto a fence or wall, train climbers along its length to maximize the impact of the display. The effect will also be to guide your eye through the lower levels of planting, encouraging it to sweep upwards as it reaches the back of the border.

Adding height to a border *continued*

Pictures clockwise from top left

New heights Using a black metal trellis for unobtrusive support, the sumptuous deep pink flowers of a clematis head skywards, elevating this raised bed display to new heights. You can link one raised bed to another by bridging the gap between them with an arch. This has the added advantage of lifting the arch, giving you even more height for your money.

Twiggy wigwam Annual climbers are the lightweight stars of the summer border. Simply give them a twiggy wigwam to cling to and leave them to wend their way upwards. Make sure the flowers are within easy reach for cutting because the more blooms you pick, the more flowers are produced. This wigwam is barely visible under its floral companion of red sweet peas (*Lathyrus odoratus*) and makes a beautiful focal point in the cottage-garden-style border.

Vertical accent A fast-growing golden hop (*Humulus lupulus* 'Aureus') rapidly engulfs a pillar support to add a striking vertical accent to this yellow-themed border. Its pale foliage is the ideal backdrop to the border's lower-growing plants. For even greater visual impact, add two or more pillars and dot them around the border.

In easy reach Not all height in the border needs to be up touching the clouds. Construct a rustic arch or simple support that will present scented blooms at nose height, so that when you inspect your plants, you will be met by a wall of perfume. Here, this creamy-white climbing rose is erupting into flower, releasing its summer scent where it can be fully appreciated.

Creating a screen

The majority of climbers are fast-growing and can be made into beautiful living screens throughout the garden. Perennial climbers become denser as they put on more growth each season, and they can be trained wherever you wish. Annual climbers are useful as temporary screens, making the most of the hot months but then fading away after flowering.

Pictures clockwise from top left

Low-level feature Open wooden fences can be used as climber supports to create a low-level screen. Here, passionflower (*Passiflora caerulea*), cup-and-saucer vine (*Cobaea scandens*), and a squash plant intermingle to create an unusual fruit and flower feature. This is a screen for the summer months only because the annual plants will not survive the winter.

Rose screen Push climbers up to higher levels with a tall screen of climbing roses on wooden supports. Their foliage and flowers not only make a great spectacle but also help to shade the patio from the harsh midday sun.

Picket fence Combine colourful climbers with painted fences to set one off against the other. This low, wooden picket fence is brought to life by the zingy orange flowers of the climbing nasturtium (*Tropaeolum majus*), which threads its way through the uprights.

Weather protection The suspended stems of a grape vine (*Vitis vinifera*) have been fashioned to create a secluded seating area. Such a screen will give protection both from the heat of a summer's day as well as from light showers of rain.

Flowering framework The effectiveness of this screen is due to the profuse flowering of the vigorous rose (*Rosa* Summer Breeze) laced through the latticework fence and gateway surround. A clematis injects pink highlights into the scene.

Decorating houses and buildings

Throughout history, climbing plants have been used to decorate houses and buildings. Whether for their flowers, perfume, or leaves, or a combination of all three, people have chosen climbers to enhance the look of their homes. Some climbers come into their own in autumn with a blaze of colour, while others maintain a steady show throughout spring and summer.

Pictures clockwise from top left

Inviting doorway A rustic doorway is partially obscured by a Chilean potato tree (*Solanum crispum* 'Glasnevin'). Its purple-blue flowers, which last from summer to autumn, make this entrance infinitely more inviting than a bare, unadorned one. If the climber becomes too adventurous, the stems that get in the way can simply be snipped off. It is up to you how far the climber is allowed to grow – at worst you will be sacrificing just a few flowers.

Ivy walls Boston ivy (*Parthenocissus tricuspidata*) clings to the front of this house without the need for additional support. Although green for much of the year, in autumn, this climber will transform the façade into a magnificent wall of rich fiery red (*see p.31*). Although a short display, it is one well worth waiting for.

Curtain call Around a blue gothic door, an ornamental vine (*Vitis*) is shedding its vibrant, red foliage, following an eye-catching autumn finale.

Rustic charm Rickety outbuildings can make photogenic features once a climber has set to work on them. This *Clematis* 'Nelly Moser' has begun to sneak over a slate-roofed shed, adding an appealing rustic charm to the scene. In time, the clematis will form a blanket of summer flowers over the entire roof.

Show home A quick fix for a timber dog kennel has been achieved by trailing a climbing nasturtium (*Tropaeolum majus*) over the roof. This is a lightweight climber that will not damage the kennel. The present occupant appears quite pleased with his recently decorated show home.

Decorating houses and buildings *continued*

Pictures clockwise from top left

Wisteria tresses One of the most beautiful sights on any building must surely be that of a wisteria in full flower. The tumbling tresses of mauve, pea-like flowers in spring or summer cannot fail to turn heads. Wisteria can be trained around windows and doors but needs a strong support because its stems become woody and heavy with age. Kept close to the wall, this wisteria has put on a striking spring display to complement the pink tulips planted below.

Window frame The advantage of growing climbers around a window is that they can be appreciated from both indoors and out. This Boston ivy (*Parthenocissus tricuspidata*) will create a stained-glass window effect if viewed from indoors on a sunny day. Since it is self-clinging, Boston ivy requires little input from the owner other than to control its exuberance.

Foliage façade Careful pruning has ensured that this *Hedera helix* 'Buttercup' is allowed to flourish only where it is wanted. Regular trimming will help to encourage denser, bushier growth, which will improve the climber's appearance.

Enticing doorway Who can resist a climbing rose around a doorway? Here, a yellow rose has turned an already interesting entrance into something quite special. Regular pruning is necessary, however, to keep roses, as well as other climbers, within bounds: left to their own devices, many will become rampant and out of control.

Climbers as ground cover

Climbers can also perform very well as ground cover – many will sprawl over the soil or low-lying structures to make interesting garden features. One of the best and most adaptable climbers for this purpose is ivy (*Hedera*), which will perform well in numerous situations.

Pictures clockwise from top left

Green carpet Climbers tolerant of dry, shady conditions are to be welcomed in the garden. The ivy *Hedera colchica* 'Sulphur Heart' is proving its worth here by covering an area of bare earth at the base of a tree. Ivy produces roots along the length of its stems, so be prepared to pull out or cut off any that grow where they are not wanted. As long as the area is not in complete shade, plant bulbs, such as daffodils (*Narcissus*) or tulips (*Tulipa*), beneath the green carpet. This will ensure you have a burst of colour in spring displayed against a neutral-coloured backdrop.

Floral tree surround Allow your clematis to lie on the ground and see how it responds. This *Clematis* 'Nelly Moser' doesn't seem to care that it has nothing to climb up – it is flowering quite happily at the base of a tree trunk, brightening up a dull patch of ground. If you combine two or more clematis varieties around a tree or even the legs of a pergola or old tree stumps, you will create a pleasing patchwork effect. Alternatively, lace a clematis through a border or experiment with other climbers to see which ones work for you. At worst, you may have to replant the climber somewhere more appropriate to its needs.

Ivy balustrade Lining both sides of this flight of steps with ivy (*Hedera*) has created two low, elongated mounds. Grown in this way, the ivy has softened the hard lines of the steps and helps to focus the eye on the scene beyond. This ivy would also be effective lining the edges of a pathway or patio, or you could create a pattern by alternating a pale-leaved variety with a dark-leaved one. Keep the ivies clipped and within bounds to maintain their visual impact.

Planting and supports

Climbers use a number of different methods to scale vertical surfaces or thread their way through host trees and shrubs. In this chapter, discover how your chosen plants climb, and what types of support are best for them. To ensure your climbers get off to a good start, follow the simple steps on how to plant perennials and shrubs in different situations. You can also try sowing annual seeds to create a tower of summer flowers. In addition, step-by-step guides show how to erect and plant up a rose arch, and make a large obelisk for clematis and jasmine.

How climbers climb

Climbing plants employ a range of strategies to enable them to cling to nearby supports. By identifying which method each plant uses, you can provide the most appropriate support. Boston ivy (*Parthenocissus tricuspidata*), for instance, is happy to scale a wall using its adhesive pads alone, while a climbing rose would need additional assistance.

Yellow *Rosa* Graham Thomas mingling with a white clematis

Stem roots

The stem roots of ivy (*Hedera* species) have a tenacious grip and cling tightly to almost any surface. The roots grow from points all along the stems, and enable ivies to scale bare brick or stone walls, or the trunks of trees where they press themselves into the smallest of gaps and fissures. Old crumbling mortar may be dislodged by climbers with this type of root sytem.

Other examples of climbers with stem roots are *Ficus*, *Pileostegia*, and *Schizophragma*.

Hedera canariensis 'Ravensholst'

Adhesive pads

Plants that climb using adhesive pads are most commonly seen covering vast expanses of vertical walls. The adapted tendrils of climbers such as Boston ivy (*Parthenocissus tricuspidata*) have small clusters of adhesive pads at their tips, which cling on to almost any surface they come into contact with. Climbers that employ this method are quite capable of covering bare walls without help, after initial support for the young stems has been provided.

Other examples of climbers that use adhesive pads include *Parthenocissus quinquefolia* and *P. henryana*.

Parthenocissus tricuspidata

Leaf stalk and tendril twiners

Many climbers use twining leaf stalks or tendrils to gain height. The leaf stalks of clematis curl around and hold on to trellis or supporting shrubs or trees. The stem tendrils of vines (*Vitis*) and the leaf tendrils of sweet peas (*Lathyrus odoratus*) will twine around and cling to an obelisk or wigwam, or twist around twigs or small branches.

Other examples are *Rhodochiton atrosanguineus*, which uses leaf stalks to climb, passionflower (*Passiflora*), which clings with stem tendrils, and the cup and saucer vine (*Cobaea scandens*), which uses leaf tendrils.

Clematis 'Bees' Jubilee'

Stem twiners

The majority of climbing plants climb by twining their stems around supports; some cling more strongly than others. A strong stem twiner is wisteria, whose permanent stems become thick and woody with time. Some twiners are less vigorous and may need a little help to gain purchase. *Berberidopsis* benefits from plenty of extra support for its loosely twining stems, while honeysuckle (*Lonicera* species) will seek out its own suitable support.

Other examples of stem-twining climbers are the hop (*Humulus lupulus*), star jasmine (*Trachelospermum*), and the annual morning glory (*Ipomoea*).

Lonicera periclymenum 'Serotina'

Hooks

Some plants manage to gain height using another ingenious method of climbing. *Rosa* 'Climbing Iceberg' stays aloft as it grows through trees and shrubs by hooking itself to its host with backward-curving thorns. Even though climbing roses are often also tied to supports, their thorns are still effective in helping them hold on to trellis and wires. Some bougainvillea also have hooked thorns, and use them to hold stems up as they scramble through other plants or specially provided supports.

Some species of *Rubus* (brambles) also use hooks to scramble upwards.

Rosa 'Climbing Iceberg'

Selecting the right support

Plant supports come in a wide range of shapes, sizes, and materials. Some are functional rather than pretty, but they all do the same job of providing a secure surface for climbing plants to twine up or scramble over. Here is a selection of some of the more common structures.

Simple spirals

Elegant metal spirals are ideal for supporting lightweight climbers in pots or confined spaces. Even where a support is visible, the clean-cut lines can be a bonus, adding to the modern feel in a contemporary display.

Suitable plants Small clematis, sweet peas (*Lathyrus odoratus*), and *Sollya heterophylla*.

Multi-purpose trellis

Wooden trellis is a commonly used form of climbing plant support. It is versatile and can be used against a wall, or as a screen or division within a garden, while still allowing air and light to pass through. Trellis can be painted or stained to match a colour scheme. Climbers may secure themselves to the woodwork; garden twine or ties can also be used.

Suitable plants Climbing roses, clematis, honeysuckle (*Lonicera*), and passionflower (*Passiflora*). Annual climbers, such as morning glory (*Ipomoea*), will also do well.

Invisible support

Climbers can be discreetly supported using a system of wires fanned out and secured to a fence or wall with nails or screw-eyes. Once the plant is established, it is virtually impossible to detect the means by which it is held aloft. This system works well for wall-trained shrubs, too, such as the Californian lilac (*Ceanothus*) shown right.

Suitable plants Spreading climbers such as honeysuckle (*Lonicera*), jasmine (*Jasminum officinale*), passionflower (*Passiflora*), and grapevines (*Vitis*).

Elegant arches

Arches enable you to walk through a floral display, so it is worth choosing good-quality wood or metal designs that will add to the overall effect. Climbers with scent as well as colour make good choices for arches – roses have long been favoured for the perfumed display they offer. Ensure the arch is strong enough to take the weight of heavy plants.

Suitable plants Climbing roses, clematis, honeysuckle (*Lonicera*), star jasmine (*Trachelospermum*), and combinations of climbers including annuals.

Shady pergolas

Pergolas generally make the largest and sturdiest of climbing supports and are capable of supporting the heavier and woodier climbing plants. Pergolas provide shade over paths and seating areas and, when smothered in plants, have a lot to offer in terms of flowers, scent, foliage, or fruit. Large climbers will need to be tied to metal fixings to secure them, making them safe for anyone walking beneath.

Suitable plants Wisteria, climbing roses, hops (*Humulus lupulus*), vines (*Vitis*), and honeysuckle (*Lonicera*).

Ornamental obelisks

Made of metal, timber, or woven willow or hazel, obelisks are generally used to add height to displays. Annuals and perennials will be equally at home, and the structure can easily be moved at the end of the season. Try growing some kitchen garden plants up an obelisk, like the runner beans shown here.

Suitable plants Clematis, climbing roses, jasmine (*Jasminum officinale*), sweet peas (*Lathyrus odoratus*), black-eyed Susan (*Thunbergia alata*), morning glory (*Ipomoea*), and climbing beans.

Adding extra support

Climbers often require extra support once they have settled in and begun to send out vigorous young shoots. You can help by providing them with wires, trellis, or netting to meet their needs.

Wiring on a house wall Wiring against a house wall usually takes the form of a series of evenly spaced horizontal wires to create a strong, but unobtrusive framework. Wires may also be fixed to make a fan shape, widening as it increases in height, or a series of vertical lines, ideal for lightweight annual climbers.

Attach wires to wood with sturdy metal screw eyes or, if you are dealing with a brick wall, use metal "vine eyes". These pins have a hole through which to secure the wire, and they can be screwed into the mortar between the bricks.

Netting and trellis Most walls and fences can be turned into "climbing frames" with plastic or wire netting, or wooden trellis. A criss-cross network is ideal for a range of climbers. Netting can also be secured between two wooden supports to make a freestanding frame. Wooden trellis panels are sturdier than netting and can support heavier climbers. Make sure panels are securely attached.

Freestanding supports When planting a climber, such as a clematis, against a wall or freestanding sturdy obelisk, it may need some help to find its way onto its main support. To ensure it grows away well, insert a bamboo cane into the planting hole and angle it onto the support. Tie the climber to the cane with garden twine, which can be removed when the plant has gained a secure purchase.

Fixing wires to a pergola

1 At the top of each pergola support, twist in four metal screw eyes, spacing them apart evenly. Repeat this at the bottom and in the centre of each support, ensuring the screw eyes are vertically aligned.

2 Thread a length of plastic-covered wire through a screw eye at the top and twist it around the vertical wire to secure. Thread the loose end through the corresponding screw eyes, pull taut and twist. Snip off any excess.

3 Here, a clematis is being tied to individual wires with soft garden twine. Twirling the climber around the support and tying it in will ensure maximum coverage with foliage and flowers. Keep tying in as the plant grows up.

Create a trellis screen

One of the best ways of providing support for climbing plants is to put up a sturdy trellis. It allows plants to be viewed from different angles, is easy to build, and creates a leafy screen.

1 Measure and mark the positions for the posts. Hammer the metal post supports into the ground with a club hammer. Use a special insert to avoid damaging the post supports as they are driven into the soil.

2 Place a wooden trellis post into the top of the metal post support and use a spirit level to check that it is vertical. It is wise to check the level on more than one side to ensure accuracy. Repeat with the other post and support.

3 Ask someone to hold each post steady and upright as you tighten the nuts on the post support with two spanners – this will hold the wooden posts firmly in place. Check that the posts are vertical once more with a spirit level.

4 Place the trellis panel in between the posts and secure it in place with screws fastened with an electric screwdriver. Check that the trellis is firmly positioned. If the trellis and posts are untreated, paint them with a wood preservative.

Build a rose arch

A garden arch is the perfect framework for your favourite climbing roses. Train roses and other climbers over it to create a focal point, and to fill your garden with perfume and colour.

1 Lay out the different pieces from the rose arch kit on the ground. Construct the top by aligning the five short cross pieces so that they slot into the two long cross beams. Use a tape measure to check they are evenly spaced.

2 Join the sections of the arch together using screws and an electric screwdriver. Galvanized screws are best for this because they do not rust, which ensures that your rose arch will last for many years to come.

3 Stand the completed rose arch in its final position and mark out where the four uprights touch the soil. With a spade, dig four holes for the legs, 45cm (18in) deep and approximately 30cm (12in) in diameter.

4 Tip some hardcore into each hole to make a solid base for the legs to stand on. A depth of about 5cm (2in) of hardcore will be sufficient. Tamp it down with a length of wood to make sure it is level and firm.

Build a rose arch *continued*

5 With help, lift the completed rose arch into place, lowering it into the holes. Make sure each leg is standing on its hardcore base. Add or remove hardcore as required until all legs are solidly supported.

6 Use a spirit level to make sure that all verticals are correctly aligned and that all horizontal pieces of the arch are level. If necessary, gently manoeuvre the structure until you are happy with its position.

7 To each hole, add some more hardcore and then ready-mixed post-mix to fill the hole up to ground level. Ensure that the post-mix completely surrounds the legs by pushing it into place with a gloved hand or piece of wood.

8 Carefully add water to the holes so that the post-mix is completely soaked. You may have to come back to each hole in turn until sufficient water has been added. Allow the post-mix to set and harden.

9 When the post-mix has set hard, you are ready to plant some roses. Dig a hole 30cm (12in) away from the outside edge of one of the posts. Place your rose, still in its pot, into the hole and use a cane to check the planting depth.

10 Mix some multipurpose compost with the soil you have removed from the hole. Take the rose out of its pot and place it in the hole at 45° to the arch. Plant it about 2.5cm (1in) deeper than the knobbly grafting point on the stem.

11 Use a spade to fill in the planting hole with the compost and soil you have just mixed. It is important that there are no air gaps around the rose's roots, so make sure the soil is crumbly with no big lumps in it.

12 Once the hole has been filled, use your foot to press the soil down firmly around the plant. Water the rose in well. Prune the stems back to strong buds, using secateurs, to encourage vigorous growth.

Planting a climber on a fence

Brighten up the fences in your garden by clothing them with colourful climbers, such as honeysuckle (*Lonicera*), which also offers a rich fragrance, perfect for balmy summer evenings spent outdoors.

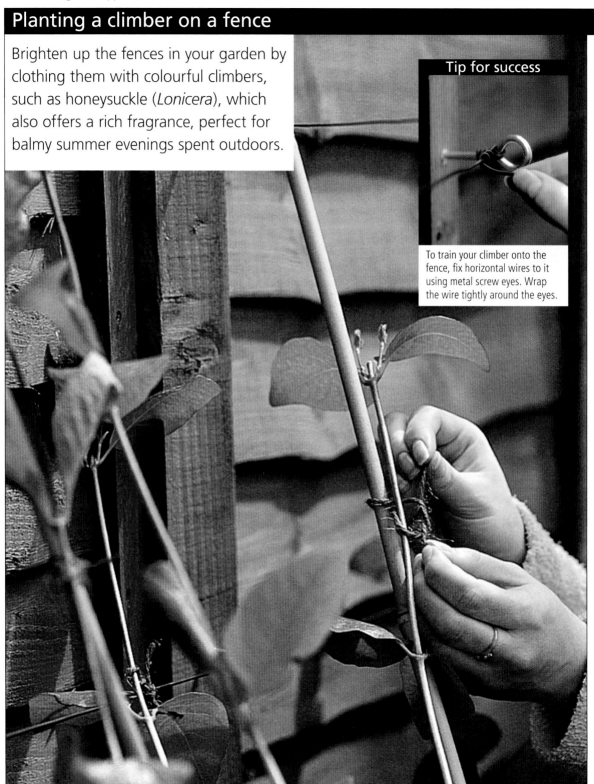

Tip for success

To train your climber onto the fence, fix horizontal wires to it using metal screw eyes. Wrap the wire tightly around the eyes.

1 Dig a hole twice the diameter of the root ball, 30–40cm (12–16in) from the fence. To support the stems and achieve good initial coverage, construct a fan from canes pushed into the soil and angled towards the fence.

2 Take the plant carefully out of its pot and place it in the hole at a 45° angle. Ensure the soil level around the plant base is the same as it was when in its pot. Gently tease out the stems and fan them out against the canes.

3 Fill the hole with the soil you previously removed, creating a slight depression around the base of the plant to aid watering. Firm the soil around the stem, removing any air pockets, and water in well to ensure the roots are soaked.

4 Tie the fanned stems loosely to the canes and horizontal wires using soft garden twine. Finally, place a layer of bark mulch around the plant. This will help to retain moisture around the roots and suppress weeds.

Make a tripod for climbing flowers

For a majestic display, grow jasmine and clematis together up a purpose-made tripod. As the plants grow, they will intertwine and look breathtaking. Create your own tripod by following these steps.

1 Decide where your tripod is to stand and dig a hole for the clematis in the centre, about 30cm (12in) deep and 30cm (12in) across. Loosen the soil at the bottom of the hole by forking it over to the depth of the fork head.

2 Add some garden compost to the planting hole along with some granular fertilizer, applied according to the manufacturer's instructions. This will help the climber to get established more quickly.

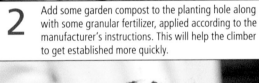

3 Check that the hole is the correct depth by placing the clematis, still in its pot, into the hole and laying a cane across it – the clematis should be planted deeply, about 5cm (2in) below the level it was at in its pot.

4 Water the pot thoroughly and carefully remove the plant by tipping the pot upside down and then tapping it to loosen the plant. Slide the plant out. Tease apart any compacted roots gently with your fingers.

Make a tripod for climbing flowers *continued*

5 Place the clematis in the hole, taking care not to damage the stems, and backfill, using the soil that you dug out earlier. With a spade, tip soil evenly around the root ball, making sure there are no large air pockets.

6 Firm the soil around the root ball. If your foot sinks, fill in with more soil, but leave a slight depression around the base of the stems to help with watering. Leave the canes in place until the tripod is in position.

7 Push three sturdy tripod supports firmly into the soil at an angle so that they form a triangle shape on the ground, centred directly over the clematis. Tie the supports together securely at the top with strong garden string.

8 Tie string around the tripod lower down for extra stability (*see p.50*) and support for the climbers. Plant a jasmine (*Jasminum officinale*) at the base of each tripod leg, following the steps shown for a honeysuckle (*see p.49*).

Tip for success

To suppress weeds and conserve moisture, mulch around the tripod and plants with a thick layer of bark chips or similar material.

9 Push bamboo canes into the soil at the centre of the tripod and angle each one to a support. Tie a stem of the clematis to each cane with soft garden twine. Also tie in the jasmine to the tripod and strings.

Potting up climbers

Climbers are well suited to growing in pots. Simply provide them with suitable supports and, once they have settled in, their flower displays will add another level of interest to your patio.

1 Place pieces of old broken flowerpot or chunks of polystyrene at the base of your pot to help water drain through the holes. Add a layer of loam-based compost, and then position the support towards the back of the pot.

2 Part-fill the pot with more compost and sit the climber on top, to check that it will be at the correct level once planted. Remove the plant from its pot and place it on top of the compost, with the stems angled towards the trellis.

3 Fill around the plant with compost and lightly firm it with your hand. Ensure there is a gap of 5cm (2in) from the soil to the rim of the pot. Then fan out the stems and tie each one to the support with soft garden twine.

4 Add a layer of gravel or stones around the plant on the surface of the compost for decoration and also to help keep the climber's roots moist. Then water the plant in well using an upturned rose spray.

Sowing annuals from seed

Give your annual climbers a head start by sowing them in pots first. If you sow them in autumn, by late spring they will be large enough to be planted outdoors where you want them to flower.

Use perlite to cover fine seed that needs light to germinate. Perlite allows in light and keeps the seeds moist.

1 Use new or clean flowerpots and fill each one to the rim with seed compost. Press the compost gently with the bottom of another pot to give a level surface, approximately 1.5cm (½in) below the pot's rim.

2 Stand the pots in a tray of water and leave them until the surface of the compost becomes moist. Alternatively, water the compost carefully with a watering can fitted with a fine rose.

3 Sow seeds on the surface of the compost, spacing them out equally. A 9cm (3½in) pot is large enough for 6–10 seeds. Cover the seeds with sieved compost to the depth given on the seed packet.

4 Finally, clearly label each pot with the name of the seeds you have sown and the sowing date. The pots can then be placed on a windowsill or greenhouse shelf to allow the seeds to germinate.

Planting hardy annuals in a pot

Cheap to buy and easy to grow, hardy annual climbers will erupt into a blaze of colour in summer. Plant them in pots, so that they can be placed on the patio or in other parts of the garden where a vibrant display of flowers will be appreciated.

1 Place crocks or polystyrene chunks over the drainage holes of the pot and fill with multi-purpose compost. Insert a ring of sticks or canes, evenly spaced, around the inside edge of the pot.

2 Gather the sticks together in a bundle at the very top and tie them by looping lengths of raffia or garden twine around them and securing with a knot. This will form a kind of wigwam for the plants to climb up.

3 Carefully remove the seedlings from their pots by tipping the pots upside down and splaying your fingers so that the plants do not fall out. Tease individual plants apart and lay each one next to a stick ready for planting.

4 Using your hand or a small trowel, make a small hole and plant the seedlings around the container, allocating one to each upright cane. Firm the compost around the plants, taking care not to damage them, and water in well.

Make an ivy topiary ball

You don't have to wait years to create your own topiary sculpture if you use ivy and a purpose-made frame. Here, a simple "ivy lollipop" has been created in a patio pot in just a few easy steps.

Tip for success

Nail two pieces of wood together in the shape of a cross, and brace horizontally in the pot to support the "lollipop" stem.

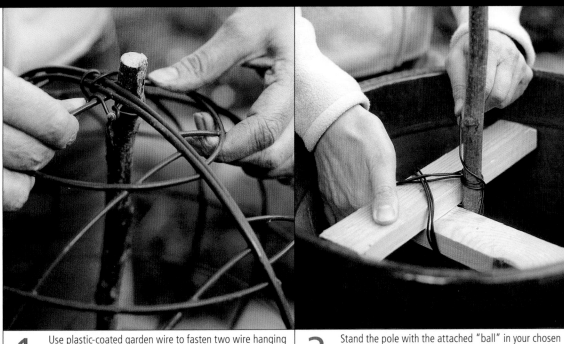

1   Use plastic-coated garden wire to fasten two wire hanging baskets together to form the shape of a ball. Suspend the ball from a nail banged into a sturdy wooden pole 1.2m (4ft) long. Use more wire to hold it in position.

2   Stand the pole with the attached "ball" in your chosen container and secure it with wire to a wooden, cross-shaped wedge fitted near the pot rim. Ensure the pole is kept perfectly vertical.

3   Place a layer of crocks or broken polystyrene pieces in the bottom of the pot and fill it up with multi-purpose compost. Plant three ivy (Hedera helix) plants around the central pole and water in well.

4   Help the ivy to climb by tying stems to the pole with garden twine. Once they reach the hanging-basket ball, weave the stems in and out so that they cover the surface. Once established, trim regularly to maintain the shape.

Climbing combinations

Mixing climbers with other plants to produce exciting displays can be a challenge, so to help you, the recipes in this chapter provide a range of inspirational planting combinations. The symbols below are used in the recipes to show the growing conditions preferred by each plant.

Key to plant symbols

♗   Plants given the RHS Award of Garden Merit

Soil preference

○   Well-drained soil

◖   Moist soil

●   Wet soil

Preference for sun or shade

☀   Full sun

☼   Partial or dappled shade

☀   Full shade

Hardiness ratings

✳✳✳   Fully hardy plants

✳✳   Plants that survive outside in mild regions or sheltered sites

✳   Plants that need protection from frost over winter

✹   Tender plants that do not tolerate any degree of frost

Rustic arch

Traditional rustic arches can be easily fashioned from lengths of tree branch nailed together. They are usually strong and make sturdy structures for climbing roses and other heavy climbers. This rustic arch is adorned with a climbing rose, honeysuckle (*Lonicera*), and clematis to make an attractive opening in the picket fence. A range of lower-growing plants, including lady's mantle (*Alchemilla mollis*), catmint (*Nepeta* x *faassenii*), and delphiniums, camouflage, and give colour to, the bottom of the arch.

Border basics

Size 1.5mx60cm (5x2ft)

Suits Division between different garden "rooms" or over a garden gate

Soil Any but not waterlogged or overly dry

Site Sunny or partially shady

Shopping list

- 2 x *Rosa* 'Cécile Brünner'
- 4 x blue delphiniums
- 6 x *Alchemilla mollis*
- 2 x *Clematis* 'Savannah'
- 1 x *Lonicera* x *heckrottii*
- 3 x *Nepeta* x *faassenii*

Planting and aftercare

After fixing the arch securely in position, place a rose and a clematis at the foot of each upright. Dig holes approximately 30cm (12in) apart and place the plants in their respective holes, leaning them towards the arch to help them on their way. Tie the stems to the wooden structure, spacing them out for maximum coverage. Repeat the process on the other side of the arch. Plant the honeysuckle, in the same way, close to the fence. As it grows, allow it to mix with the other climbers on the arch. Finally, plant the lower-growing plants around the outside of the arch. Water all plants in well and tie in climbers when their stems become overly long.

Rosa 'Cécile Brünner'
✾✾✾ ◐ ◊ ☼ ◑ ♉

Blue delphinium
✾✾✾ ◊ ☼

Alchemilla mollis
✾✾✾ ◐ ◊ ☼ ◑ ♉

Clematis 'Savannah'
✾✾✾ ◐ ◊ ☼

Lonicera x heckrottii
✾✾✾ ◐ ◊ ☼ ◑

Nepeta x faassenii
✾✾✾ ◊ ☼ ◑ ♉

Pink confection for an obelisk

Taking the time to colour-theme your planting is worth the effort because the end result will be more striking than a hotchpotch group of plants. This display includes pink roses and perennials, with white delphiniums to introduce light into the group. The two roses, although not climbers or ramblers, have been encouraged to envelop a metal obelisk to provide height to the scheme, while the astrantias, *Thalictrum*, and ice plant (*Sedum spectabile*) continue the colour theme at a lower level.

Border basics

Size 3x2m (10x6ft)

Suits Cottage garden, informal borders

Soil Any, except waterlogged or very dry

Site Sunny/partial shade

Shopping list

- 1 x *Rosa* 'William Lobb'
- 2 x *Thalictrum aquilegiifolium*
- 3 x white delphiniums
- 1 x *Rosa* 'Reine Victoria'
- 2 x *Sedum spectabile*
- 3 x *Astrantia* 'Hadspen Blood'

Planting and aftercare

First, mark out the planting area, then enrich the soil by forking in well-rotted manure or garden compost.

Site the metal obelisk where it will be most visible, taking care not to obscure lower-growing plants. Plant both roses close to the obelisk and tie in their stems to the support. Position the lower-growing plants evenly around the roses, allowing room for them to expand as they grow. Water the display thoroughly once planted and keep the soil moist to allow the roots to settle in.

Regular feeding shouldn't be necessary except on very light or sandy soils. Apply a mulch of garden compost around plants to suppress weeds, conserve moisture, and provide a steady supply of nutrients.

Rosa 'William Lobb'
❄❄❄ ◗ ◌ ☼ ♈

White delphinium
❄❄❄ ◗ ◌ ☼

Sedum spectabile
❄❄❄ ◗ ◌ ☼ ♈

Thalictrum aquilegiifolium
❄❄❄ ◗ ◌ ◐

Rosa 'Reine Victoria'
❄❄❄ ◗ ◌ ☼

Astrantia 'Hadspen Blood'
❄❄❄ ◗ ◌ ☼ ◐

Elegant seating

Garden seating provides the perfect setting to soak up the surrounding atmosphere and admire your garden. You can also make it into a feature with a selection of carefully chosen plants. Climbers are ideal for providing a living curtain of colour, as the green-yellow foliage of the hop (*Humulus lupulus* 'Aureus') does here, while the white blooms of the rose (*Rosa* 'Climbing Iceberg') and the mauve clematis (*Clematis* 'Lasurstern') trained over an arch, create a colourful roof. Clumps of catmint (*Nepeta sibirica*) provide vibrant colour at ground level.

Border basics

Size   3x1.5m (10x5ft)

Suits   Large or small garden

Soil   Any, but not waterlogged or very dry

Site   Full sun or partial shade

Shopping list

- 2 x *Clematis* 'Lasurstern'
- 2 x *Rosa* 'Climbing Iceberg'
- 2 x *Humulus lupulus* 'Aureus'
- 6 x *Nepeta sibirica*

Planting and aftercare

Once you have positioned the seat and erected an arch over it, you are ready to plant. Fork in some garden compost or well-rotted manure into the soil and plant two golden hops behind the seat against a trellis or on horizontal wires attached to the wall. On either side of the arch plant a rose and a clematis, tying in their stems to the support to encourage them to grow in the right direction. Plant two lines of catmint alongside the path leading to the seat.

The roses will need tying in at intervals to keep them tight against the support, and the hops may need clipping back to stop them becoming too invasive. If required, clip the catmint back from the path after flowering.

Clematis 'Lasurstern'
❋❋❋ ◍ ◌ ☼ ☼ ♀

Rosa 'Climbing Iceberg'
❋❋❋ ◍ ◌ ☼ ♀

Humulus lupulus 'Aureus'
❋❋❋ ◍ ◌ ☼ ☼ ♀

Nepeta sibirica
❋❋❋ ◍ ◌ ☼ ☼

Cottage garden combination

This combination of climbers and herbaceous plants lends itself perfectly to a cottage-garden display. It is compact enough to slip in at the end of a border, close to a wall or house, especially if the planting is mirrored on either side of a pathway. As the clematis and rose mature, the effect will become more striking as the foliage and flowers intertwine, providing a long-lasting summer display of colour.

Border basics

Size 3x2m (10x6ft)
Suits Herbaceous borders, informal gardens
Soil Most soils, but not waterlogged or overly dry
Site Full sun or partial shade

Shopping list

- 1 x *Clematis* 'Arabella'
- 1 x *Rosa* x *odorata* 'Mutabilis'
- 6 x *Alstroemeria*
- 3 x *Helenium* 'Moerheim Beauty'

Planting and aftercare

If the soil requires it, add some well-rotted manure or garden compost before planting. Plant the rose towards the back of the display and place the wigwam in front, leaving sufficient space around it for the alstroemerias and heleniums. Then plant the clematis at the base of the wigwam, twining the shoots around the support. Next, plant the heleniums and alstroemerias on either side of the wigwam, making sure they have enough room to spread. Water everything in well.

To prolong the rose's flowering period, remove the spent blooms as soon as they begin to fade. Look out, too, for signs of pests or disease, and treat anything suspicious immediately.

Hard prune the clematis to a pair of strong buds in spring each year.

Clematis 'Arabella'
❄❄ ◐ ○ ☼ ♥

Rosa x *odorata* 'Mutabilis'
❄❄❄ ◐ ○ ☼ ◑ ♥

Alstroemeria
❄❄ ◐ ○ ☼ ◑

Helenium 'Moerheim Beauty'
❄❄❄ ◐ ○ ☼ ♥

Blazing autumn screen

Gardens often flower freely during the summer, leaving nothing to enjoy at the end of the season, but by choosing your plants carefully, you can retain the interest for much longer. Here, an ornamental vine (*Vitis coignetiae*) and Boston ivy (*Parthenocissus tricuspidata*) have put on their fiery autumnal colours to disguise a dull wall and old shed, and provide an eye-catching backdrop to the asters, *Stachys*, and chrysanthemums.

Border basics

Size 2x2m (6x6ft)

Suits Any position with a wall or fence as a backdrop

Soil Most soils, but not waterlogged or overly dry

Site Corner of garden, border in front of wall in full sun or partial shade

Shopping list

- 1 x Boston ivy (*Parthenocissus tricuspidata*)
- 1 x *Rosa* 'Bobbie James'
- 1 x *Stachys byzantina*
- 1 x *Vitis coignetiae*
- 2 x orange chrysanthemums
- 2 x yellow chrysanthemums
- 3 x *Aster* x *frikartii* 'Mönch'

Planting and aftercare

Plant the Boston ivy about 45cm (18in) away from the base of a wall, fence, or trellis. It is self-clinging, but a few bamboo canes leant against the wall will help it to get started. The asters can be planted directly into the ground alongside the chrysanthemums, or the latter could be grown in terracotta pots to provide an extra element of interest.

Water in after planting and during prolonged dry spells. Prune overly long stems of the climbers when necessary, and deadhead the chrysanthemums and asters throughout the flowering season.

Parthenocissus tricuspidata
❋❋❋ ◊ ☼ ♉

Rosa 'Bobbie James'
❋❋❋ ◗ ◊ ☼ ♉

Stachys byzantina
❋❋❋ ◊ ☼

Vitis coignetiae
❋❋❋ ◊ ☼ ◐ ♉

Chrysanthemum (orange and yellow)
❋❋❋ ◗ ◊ ☼

Aster x *frikartii* 'Mönch'
❋❋❋ ◊ ☼ ♉

Tree decked with pink garlands

A theme based on warm colours binds together this varied mix of plants. The striking centrepiece, the compact conifer *Abies*, is bedecked with the annual climber *Rhodochiton*, with its garlands of pink and mauve parachute flowers. Around its base, dahlias and *Sedum* provide a splash of colour.

The lightweight twining stems of the *Rhodochiton* will not harm the conifer, even though they can cover a significant surface area in summer. In late summer and early autumn, the large pink flowerheads of the *Sedum* will attract butterflies and hoverflies.

Border basics

Size 2x2m (6x6ft)

Suits Informal border or island bed

Soil Well drained, moderately fertile

Site Full sun or partial shade

Shopping list

- 1 x *Abies lasiocarpa* var. *arizonica* 'Compacta'
- 2 x *Rhodochiton atrosanguineus*
- 3 x *Dahlia* 'Grenadier'
- 3 x *Sedum* 'Herbstfreude'

Planting and aftercare

The largest component of this scheme is the *Abies*, which provides an evergreen backdrop for the colourful plants surrounding it. Site the conifer first, towards the back of the border, then arrange the *Sedum* in front of the dahlias, leaving a little space near the conifer for the *Rhodochiton*. This tender plant is grown from seed and planted out in late spring after the frosts. Or grow it in a pot and tuck it behind the *Sedum*, allowing the stems to scramble through the conifer. Remove the climber's dead stems in late autumn.

In most areas, the dahlia tubers should be lifted after flowering and stored in a frost-free shed until spring.

Abies lasiocarpa var. *arizonica* 'Compacta' ❄❄❄ ◐ ◊ ☼ ♚

Rhodochiton atrosanguineus ❄ ◐ ◊ ☼ ♚

Dahlia 'Grenadier' ❄ ◐ ◊ ☼ ♚

Sedum 'Herbstfreude' ❄❄❄ ◐ ◊ ☼ ♚

Vine entrance

Entrances to different parts of the garden can be made more attractive by the clever use of plants. Covered with an edible grapevine (*Vitis vinifera*) and ivy (*Hedera*), and underplanted with a hosta, sedge (*Carex*), fern (*Dryopteris*), and New Zealand flax (*Phormium*), this wooden doorway has been transformed into a leafy focal point. The varied mix of foliage shapes and colours more than makes up for the lack of brightly coloured flowers.

Border basics

Size 3x1m (10x3ft)

Suits Any garden with separate "rooms" or planting styles

Soil Any moist but well-drained soil

Site Full sun for the vine; partial shade for the lower-growing plants

Shopping list

- 1 x *Vitis vinifera*
- 1 x *Hedera helix*
- 1 x *Dryopteris affinis*
- 1 x *Carex flagellifera*
- 1 x *Hosta* 'Golden Prayers'
- 1 x *Phormium*

Planting and aftercare

Establish the vine and ivy on the wooden framework before planting the non-climbing plants. Train, and initially tie in, the stems of the vine onto one side of the entrance, while allowing the ivy to cling to the uprights on the other side. Arrange the other plants according to size, with the hosta at the front. As these plants mature, their foliage will mask any hard path edges.

Keep the plants well watered. The hosta and fern will particularly enjoy a moist, slightly shady position. Don't waterlog the soil, however, or allow it to become dry to the touch. Each winter surround the plants with a mulch of well-rotted manure or garden compost.

Vitis vinifera
✽✽✽ ◐ ◊ ☼ ◑

Hedera helix
✽✽✽ ◐ ◊ ☼ ◑

Dryopteris affinis
✽✽✽ ◐ ◊ ◑ ♈

Carex flagellifera
✽✽✽ ◐ ◊ ☼ ◑

Hosta 'Golden Prayers'
✽✽✽ ◐ ◊ ☼ ◑

Phormium
✽✽ ◐ ◊ ☼

Matching colours on a pergola

By colour-theming plants on and around a pergola, you ensure that similar or matching hues harmonize. Either place all warm colours together, with cool colours separate or, as here, mix opposing but complementary hues. Try a yellow rambling rose (*Rosa banksiae* 'Lutea') with a mauve clematis (*Clematis* 'Elsa Späth') and purple-flowered magnolia (*Magnolia liliiflora* 'Nigra') for a dramatic effect. Don't be afraid to experiment with colour. If it works for you, don't worry if it's against "the rules".

Rosa banksiae 'Lutea'
❀ ❀ ◊ ☼ ♔

Clematis 'Elsa Späth'
❀ ❀ ❀ ◊ ☼

Border basics

Size 2x1.5m (6x5ft)

Suits Wrought ironwork pergola, screen, trellis, or wall-mounted support

Soil Any, but not waterlogged or very dry

Site Full sun for clematis and roses, partially shaded for hostas

Shopping list

- 1 x *Rosa banksiae* 'Lutea'
- 1 x *Clematis* 'Elsa Späth'
- 1 x *Magnolia liliiflora* 'Nigra'
- 1 x *Hosta fortunei* var. *aureomarginata*
- 1 x *Hosta sieboldiana* var. *elegans*
- 1 x *Lamium maculatum* 'Album'

Planting and aftercare

First, plant the magnolia, clematis, and rose, attaching these last two climbers to the support with garden twine to start them growing in the right direction. The clematis will cling but the rose will need to be kept in check and re-tied to keep it within bounds. Next, plant the hostas and deadnettle (*Lamium maculatum*) at the front of the display. The hostas will thrive in a humus-rich, moist soil, so provide them with plenty of well-rotted organic matter when planting and subsequently as a top-up mulch. In spring, remove any dead and damaged stems on the clematis and reduce other stems to a pair of strong buds.

Magnolia liliiflora 'Nigra'
❀ ❀ ❀ ◊ ◊ ☼ ◑ ♔

Hosta fortunei var. *aureomarginata*
❀ ❀ ❀ ◊ ◊ ☼ ◑ ♔

Hosta sieboldiana var. *elegans*
❀ ❀ ❀ ◊ ◊ ☼ ◑ ♔

Lamium maculatum 'Album'
❀ ❀ ❀ ◊ ◊ ☼ ◑

Wall of spring scent

For gardeners, spring is a time of optimism and excitement as leaves unfurl and buds begin to break, revealing a kaleidoscope of colours and flower perfumes. Many plants have a delicate scent, which provides light fragrance in the garden without becoming overpowering. Here, the wisteria (*Wisteria* x *formosa*) provides a gentle aroma as pea-like blooms cascade from its searching stems. An added bonus is that the flowers are often at head height, so it is not necessary to bend down to appreciate them.

Border basics

Size 4x1m (12x3ft)

Suits Garden with sunny wall or sturdy wooden arbour

Soil Any soil that isn't waterlogged or overly dry

Site Sunny position

Shopping list

- 1 x *Wisteria* x *formosa*
- 1 x *Laburnum* x *watereri* 'Vossii'
- 20 x *Allium hollandicum* 'Purple Sensation' or *Tulipa* 'Queen of Night'

Planting and aftercare

The laburnum and wisteria will take a few seasons to become fully established and produce a striking flower display. Prepare the soil well where they are to be planted. Incorporate organic matter, such as garden compost, into the surrounding soil, and keep the soil moist while new roots are forming.

Plant groups of complementary spring bulbs, such as *Allium hollandicum* 'Purple Sensation', or *Tulipa* 'Queen of Night', with its velvet purple blooms, around the bases of both plants for a vibrant display. If the soil is clay or generally wet, add horticultural grit to the planting holes to prevent the bulbs from rotting.

Wisteria x *formosa*
❋❋❋ ◐ ◌ ☼ ☀

Laburnum x *watereri* 'Vossii'
❋❋❋ ◌ ☼ ♔

Allium hollandicum 'Purple Sensation' ❋❋❋ ◌ ☼ ♔

Alternative plant idea

Tulipa 'Queen of Night'
❋❋❋ ◌ ☼

Modern rustic archway

If you like a range of gardening styles and themes, there is nothing to stop you combining more than one for the best of both worlds. Here, modern chic meets rustic charm. This garden includes an archway made of bare steel rather than the more traditional wood. It has weathered to orange-brown rust and blends perfectly with the surrounding planting. Trained up one side is a star jasmine (*Trachelospermum jasminoides*), while around the base, and either side of the slate-chipping path, is a rich mix of grasses and herbaceous plants.

Solanum crispum 'Glasnevin'
❄❄ ◐ ◊ ☼ ♈

Trachelospermum jasminoides
❄❄ ◊ ☼ ◑ ♈

Border basics

Size 4x2.5m (12x8ft)

Suits Pathway leading to stand-alone feature or bench between borders

Soil Moist but not waterlogged or too dry

Site Full sun or partial shade

Shopping list

- 1 x *Solanum crispum* 'Glasnevin'
- 1 x *Trachelospermum jasminoides*
- 2 x *Stipa gigantea*
- 4 x *Leymus arenarius*
- 2 x *Echinops ritro*
- 2 x *Hosta* 'Love Pat'

Stipa gigantea
❄❄❄ ◊ ☼ ♈

Leymus arenarius
❄❄❄ ◊ ☼

Planting and aftercare

Concrete the arch firmly into the ground. Once the concrete has set, plant the star jasmine at the base of the arch on one side. Train the stems up the arch, tying them in with wire or twine. Giant feather grass (*Stipa gigantea*) and Chilean potato tree (*Solanum crispum*) have been planted near the fence to provide focal points framed by the archway.

Mix the broad-leaved hosta with the narrow-leaved *Leymus* to create a contrast of foliage shape.

Although no special soil preparation is necessary, all these plants will benefit from well-rotted manure, applied as a mulch in winter or early spring.

Echinops ritro
❄❄❄ ◊ ☼ ◑ ♈

Hosta 'Love Pat'
❄❄❄ ◐ ◊ ☼ ◑ ♈

Quick cover-up

The beauty of climbers such as Spanish flag (*Ipomoea lobata*) is that they grow so quickly. You don't have to wait years for the plant to establish before it gives a good account of itself. Grown as an annual, it will be smothered in blooms throughout the summer, providing an instant blaze of colour. It is a lightweight plant, so it can be allowed to scramble safely through smaller perennials without fear of them being damaged. For a quick cover-up, such as filling an unwanted gap in a border or disguising an unsightly compost bin, a small display like this will be enough to distract, and please, the eye.

Border basics

Size 1x1m (3x3ft)

Suits Any border with a gap or an unsightly compost bin or water butt

Soil Any well-drained soil

Site Full sun or partial shade

Shopping list

- 1 x *Ipomoea lobata* or *Tropaeolum majus* (nasturtium)
- 3 x *Verbena bonariensis*
- 3 x *Canna* 'Musifolia'

Planting and aftercare

Enrich the soil with some organic matter before planting the cannas. Set these to the back of the display, so their foliage becomes the backdrop to the flowering verbena and Spanish flag. Plant the verbena in front of the cannas in a triangle, leaving space in the middle for the Spanish flag. Alternatively, raise up the climber in an attractive pot and stand it in the middle of the verbenas. Water the border regularly in dry weather. The cannas will need plenty of moisture to prevent their large leaves wilting. In frost-prone areas, dig up the cannas and store them over winter in a frost-free place. Protect the verbenas with a straw mulch.

Ipomoea lobata
✿ ◌ ☼

Verbena bonariensis
❄❄ ◗ ◌ ☼ ♔

Canna 'Musifolia'
❄ ◌ ☼ ♔

Alternative plant idea

Tropaeolum majus
❄ ◗ ◌ ☼

Summer sunshine in a pot

Give your patio a taste of summer sun and create a striking pot display. This refreshing yellow and white palette makes an effective, eye-catching group of flowering and foliage plants. Choose plants that will give height, but also interest at a lower level. The climbing black-eyed Susan (*Thunbergia alata*) will twine its way up a wigwam, while the lax stems of the trailing snapdragon (*Antirrhinum* Trailing White) and *Senecio macroglossus* 'Variegatus' help to disguise the outline of the pot.

Container basics

Size Approx. 30cm (12in) diameter, 30cm (12in) high, terracotta pot

Suits Patio or balcony

Compost Multi-purpose potting compost

Site Full sun

Shopping list

- 1 x *Antirrhinum* 'Trailing White'
- 2 x *Petunia* 'Prism Sunshine'
- 2 x white petunias
- 1 x *Thunbergia alata*
- 3 x *Senecio macroglossus* 'Variegatus'

Planting and aftercare

Place some broken crocks or chunks of polystyrene in the bottom of the pot for drainage. Fill with multi-purpose potting compost, with some slow-release fertilizer granules, to just below the rim. Stand a 90cm (36in) high bamboo cane tripod in the centre, ensuring the legs are pushed firmly into the compost. Plant the black-eyed Susan first and twine the stems around the canes for support. Lower-growing plants can then be placed at equal intervals around the edge of the pot. Water well.

During the summer, water frequently, especially when the weather is hot. If you didn't add fertilizer to the compost when planting, water fortnightly with a liquid feed.

Antirrhinum Trailing White
❄ ◊ ☼

Petunia 'Prism Sunshine'
❄ ◊ ☼

Thunbergia alata
✿ ◊ ☼

Senecio macroglossus 'Variegatus'
✿ ◊ ☼ ♕

Climbing bells

The centrepiece of this pot display is a cascade of purple parachutes provided by the climbing stems of *Rhodochiton atrosanguineus*. A tall, dark, ceramic pot is the perfect foil for the silver-green *Cerinthe* and the trailing *Plectranthus*. Simple colour combinations, limited to silvers and purple/mauve, create a balanced display. Plants that flower at the same time create the biggest impact.

A solitary display looks good in the middle of a patio or centred against a wall, while two identical pots can be positioned as sentinels, one either side of a doorway.

Container basics

Size Approx. 45cm (18in) diameter, 55cm (22in) high, glazed ceramic pot
Suits Patio centrepiece, or alongside a door
Compost Loam-based potting compost
Site Sun or partial shade

Shopping list

- 3 x *Plectranthus zatarhendii*
- 1 x *Rhodochiton atrosanguineus* or *Sollya heterophylla*
- 2 x *Cerinthe major* 'Purpurascens'

Planting and aftercare

Place crocks or chunks of polystyrene at the base of the pot for drainage. Fill to just below the rim with multi-purpose compost mixed with slow-release fertilizer granules. Position a bamboo tripod centrally in the pot and push well into the compost. Plant the *Rhodochiton* first, guiding the young stems onto the bamboo canes. Follow this with the two *Cerinthe* and then the *Plectranthus* around the edge of the pot.

Water the compost well and, if slow-release granules were not added to the compost earlier, feed at fortnightly intervals with a proprietary liquid feed for container plants.

Plectranthus zatarhendii
❀ ◊ ☼

Rhodochiton atrosanguineus
❀ ◑ ◊ ☼ ♉

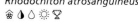
Alternative plant idea

Cerinthe major 'Purpurascens'
❀❀❀ ◊ ☼

Sollya heterophylla
❀ ◑ ◊ ☼ ◐ ♉

Pruning and propagation

Most climbing plants benefit from an annual prune, which stimulates new growth and results in stronger, healthier plants and more abundant flowers and fruit. This chapter outlines the basic pruning methods, as well as the specific pruning requirements of the most popular climbers. In addition, there are ways to make new plants from old using simple propagation techniques, such as layering and taking cuttings. Step-by-step sequences at the end of the chapter show how to propagate your plants using these methods.

Pruning and training a climbing rose on an arch

A rose that has been properly pruned to cover an arch will reward you year after year with breathtaking flower displays. Prune climbing roses in the autumn, and remember to wear protective gloves.

Before

After

This rose arch has become engulfed by a tangled mess of old and new shoots, diminishing its flowering potential. It also looks untidy and shapeless.

Vigorous stems have been pruned back and tied to the arch, while old stems have been removed. This will result in a good flower display the following summer.

1 In autumn, first remove any dead, diseased, dying, or crossing stems, to ensure you are left with only the healthiest and strongest branches. Then you can start to prune the climber to the desired shape.

2 Armed with a pair of sharp secateurs, cut each recently flowered stem back by about two-thirds to just above a strong, healthy bud. The cut should be made at an angle, so that rain will drain away from the bud.

3 On an established climbing rose, remove old, unproductive stems close to the base, using a pair of loppers or, ideally, a pruning saw to ensure a clean cut. This will stimulate the growth of new shoots.

4 Finally, tie in the pruned new growth to wire staples hammered firmly into the arch. Use adjustable plastic ties, as shown here, or garden twine fastened in a figure of eight to support the stems securely.

Pruning clematis

Clematis are pruned in one of three ways, depending on when they flower. First, check which group your clematis falls under and then follow the method prescribed.

Three types of clematis

Clematis can be sorted into three different pruning groups (*see below and right*). Most books and plant labels will tell you which group your clematis belongs to, and how and when it is best to prune.

Group 1 The clematis in this group are early flowering and require the least drastic pruning. In fact, it is not always necessary to take your secateurs to them. Group 1 clematis include *C. alpina*, *C. armandii*, *C. cirrhosa*, *C. macropetala*, and *C. montana*, and their cultivars.

Group 2 This group contains the early to mid-season, large-flowered hybrids. Light pruning is all that is needed during late winter or early spring before new shoots appear. *Clematis* 'Doctor Ruppel', *C.* 'Marie Boisselot', and *C.* 'Miss Bateman' are among the plants in this group.

Group 3 The late-season, large-flowered hybrids, as well as the later-flowering species and small-flowered hybrids, are in this group. They need pruning hard in early spring before new shoots are produced. Plants include *Clematis* x *durandii*, *C. tangutica,* and *C. rehderiana*.

Group 1

Prune clematis in this group after flowering has finished. Although the plants can be left unpruned, they will benefit from being thinned out, rewarding you with a more abundant flower display the following year.

A good tip is to remove any dead or dying wood first before pruning to shape. The main aim is to try to create an airy, open framework of stems, removing any that have formed a dense thicket. Cut the stems back to a healthy pair of buds with secateurs but, as a general rule, do not cut back too hard. You are really only "tidying up" these clematis and keeping them within bounds.

This clematis has formed a tangled mass of stems on the trellis and is ready for a tidy up.

Carefully remove unwanted stems, pruning back to a pair of healthy buds. Tie loose stems onto the trellis with twine.

Group 2

The early to mid-season, large-flowered hybrids perform best after they have been pruned. By doing so, you will give your clematis the best chance of producing large, healthy blooms.

To produce the required strong framework of stems, remove any dead, diseased, or spindly growth in late winter or early spring, before new growth has started. Cut the remaining stems back to a pair of healthy buds, to leave a well-spaced framework. For a long season of flowers, cut some stems back harder than others. The more gently pruned stems will flower on wood produced the previous year, while those pruned hard will flower later on new wood.

Group 3

Plants in this group of late-flowering clematis are possibly the easiest to prune. They can be cut down almost to ground level each year in late winter or early spring.

With a pair of secateurs, first remove dead or dying wood, taking care not to damage young shoots emerging from around the base of the plant. Then cut the remaining stems away from their support, and prune them back to a pair of strong buds at a distance of 15–30cm (6–12in) from the soil surface. These buds will produce the current season's stems, which eventually bear flowers later in the year.

Prune clematis in Group 2 down to a pair of strong healthy buds without damaging the emerging shoots.

Cut the stems of Group 3 clematis to just above ground level, to promote healthy and vigorous new growth.

Tie healthy stems with vigorous shoots onto the trellis support. Space shoots out for maximum coverage.

A half-pruned clematis shows how the emerging shoots have not been damaged. Hard pruning stimulates new stems to shoot from the base.

Pruning a climbing rose on a wall

Climbing roses will soon grow out of control if they are not pruned regularly. It is worth spending time each year removing unwanted stems and re-tying the remaining framework to its supports.

Tip for success

To prolong the flowering period of a climber, deadhead the flowers as they fade by removing them with a pair of secateurs.

1 Before making any cuts, stand back and look at the rose growing against the wall, to visualize what it will look like after pruning. You will then know which stems to remove once you have climbed the ladder.

2 In autumn or early winter, after flowering, cut out dead, diseased, or rubbing stems. Then remove any main stems that have outgrown their allotted space. Use a pair of secateurs, or a pruning saw if the branch is thick.

3 Shorten the remaining side shoots by up to two-thirds, so that they are about 15cm (6in) long. Always prune to just above an outward-facing bud, so that the new shoots grow away from, or adjacent to, the wall.

4 Reposition the main stems against the horizontal wire supports and tie them in using garden twine. You may need to hold them in position while tying, to prevent them crossing over other stems.

5 The end result should be an open framework. One stem here crosses others to fill a big gap, but it isn't close enough to rub. Mulch with well-rotted manure or garden compost around the base to conserve moisture.

Additional rose pruning and training ideas

Roses respond well to regular pruning and careful training, so it is worth finding out which regime would most benefit your plants. Before pruning, check whether your rose is a climber or a rambler.

Rose wall A weathered brick wall is the perfect prop for a cottage-style pink climbing rose. Invisible wire supports and careful pruning maintain the illusion that the rose has scrambled up the wall naturally and ensure a prolific annual display of blooms.

Pruning ramblers

Rambling roses are more vigorous than climbers, and have flexible, spreading stems, ideal for training through trees or over pergolas. Prune them after they have flowered in summer. Untie the stems to make the task easier. Take out any dead and diseased shoots, and remove up to one third of the oldest stems. Then cut back healthy side shoots to about 8cm (3in) to leave three strong buds, and re-tie the plant to its support with garden twine.

Prune side shoots to promote vigorous growth.

Training a climber on a tripod

Climbing roses make excellent subjects for training on sturdy wooden tripods. Encourage the stems to snake around the upright supports, to give as much coverage as possible. At intervals, hammer in small wire staples, which can be used as anchors for tying in the stems. In autumn or winter, once the rose has grown beyond the top of the tripod, prune back tall stems, and cut all side shoots back to three healthy buds.

Cut back over-vigorous stems to maintain shape.

Training roses over rope swags

Swags of rope are popular features for supporting climbing and rambling roses. As soon as your rose has grown tall enough to be trained horizontally, encourage the stems to twine around the rope in the direction that looks most natural. Cut back side shoots to three buds and then secure the stems in place with garden twine. Be careful not to force the stems – older growth can be quite brittle and may break.

Cut back side shoots.   Tie in loose stems.

Serpentine training over a wooden frame

For an eye-catching feature, train your rose in a serpentine fashion over a wooden frame or heavy-duty trellis. Instead of tying stems to just one side of the support, weave the stems through the gaps while they are young and flexible, and twist them back through another gap. This will provide you with flowers on both sides of the frame. In autumn or winter, cut back side shoots to three or four buds to promote flowering.

Weave rose stems through a sturdy wooden frame.

Keeping the blooms coming

Encourage repeat-flowering roses to bloom for as long as possible by removing the old flowerheads, known as deadheading, as soon as you notice them. You can either use your fingers to break off the blooms or cut them off with a pair of secateurs. Deadheading also prevents roses from making hips filled with seed, so don't deadhead roses that are not repeat-flowering if you want to enjoy a colourful autumn display.

Remove old flowerheads.   Leave flowers unpruned for hips.

Renovating old roses

After a number of years, climbing roses become woody and produce fewer flowers. The solution is to renovate them, which means cutting out the old parts of the plant and encouraging the young, vigorous stems to take over. Each year, prune one or two of the oldest stems to within 30cm (12in) of the ground over a period of two or three years, until all of the stems have been replaced. Feed the rose with a general purpose fertilizer after pruning.

Cut back the oldest stems to renovate a rose.

Pruning wisteria

There are few sights as glorious as a mature wisteria in full bloom. To help guarantee masses of flowers year after year, a wisteria needs careful pruning in summer and in winter. Follow the steps given here to see how it should be done.

Tip for success

Prune the stems that are climbing up vertical supports, to encourage the production of as many flowers as possible.

1 Left to its own devices, a wisteria will send out long, whippy stems, which by summer will become an unruly tangle. The plant will flower better the following year when pruned and trained flat against a wall or fence.

2 In late summer, about two months after flowering, prune the current year's stems back to 15cm (6in) from a main branch with a pair of secateurs, leaving no more than six leaves. Be careful not to damage the buds.

3 In winter, reduce the length of the stems that were pruned in summer to 8–10cm (3–4in), to leave two to three buds. This will encourage the formation of short side shoots that will flower the following year.

4 It is important to prune the wisteria all over, leaving a framework of shortened stems. Make sure that the branches don't break under the weight of the flowers next season by tying them securely to their supports.

Pruning tips for common climbers

Most climbers need pruning, even if it's just snipping off the odd wayward shoot. Here are some of the most common climbers with advice on when and how to prune them.

Ivy (*Hedera*) Ivy (*right*) can become quite invasive if it is not pruned regularly. It responds well to being cut and will shoot from numerous buds to make new growth.
How to prune Ivy can be trimmed at any time of year, but to avoid losing flowers, which are valuable to wildlife, cut stems back in late winter or early spring.

Common jasmine (*Jasminum officinale*) The common jasmine (*left*) will become a dense thicket in only a few seasons if it is not pruned, so it is worth spending time clipping it back into shape. For your efforts, you will be rewarded with more vigorous growth and a better flower display. Thinning out also makes it easier to spot diseases and pest infestations.
How to prune Prune once flowering has finished, first removing any dead, dying, or diseased wood. Next, cut stems that have flowered during that season back to strong buds, and remove stems that have crowded together to form an impenetrable mass. Even after pruning, you should still be left with plenty of healthy growth to give a profusion of blooms the following summer.

Honeysuckle (*Lonicera*) A real favourite for its sweet perfume, honeysuckle (*right*) can become unruly if it is not kept in check. The growth often goes skywards, with most of the leaves and flowers at the top of the plant, leaving unattractive bare stems lower down. Regular pruning encourages buds near the base to begin growing, which will help to rectify any "top-heavy" tendencies.
How to prune The best time to prune climbing honeysuckles is after flowering in late summer. For a mature, healthy plant, use a pair of shears to snip off the side shoots, encouraging growth lower down. The side shoots of smaller or younger plants should be cut back to two to three buds from a main stem. To renovate an old but still healthy plant, cut all stems back to 60cm (24in) in autumn or winter.

Passion flower (*Passiflora*) According to how it is grown, a passion flower (*right*) may or may not need pruning. If it is allowed to roam through a large tree, you can probably leave it alone. However, a wall-trained specimen will almost certainly need, and benefit from, a decent haircut. Secateurs are generally all that is required, although some shoots can get quite woody with age, in which case you may need to use a pruning saw.

How to prune Prune either straight after flowering or between late winter and early spring before the new growth starts. Cut back side shoots to within three or four buds of the main stems. For a more general tidy up, simply cut back the stems to fit the available space.

Virginia creeper and Boston ivy (*Parthenocissus*) Boston ivy (*Parthenocissus tricuspidata*) (*left*) and Virginia creeper (*P. quinquefolia*) are very fast-growing climbers. In addition, their low-growing stems will root wherever they touch the soil, resulting in plants popping up all around the garden. For this reason, pruning is particularly important, otherwise you will be inundated with unwanted plants.

How to prune Wait until the autumn foliage has fallen before pruning in early winter. Cut back very long stems and those that have extended well beyond their allotted space. Always cut back to healthy buds from which new shoots will grow. Over-exuberant summer growth can be treated in the same way.

Vine (*Vitis*) Like the Boston ivy pictured above, ornamental vines (*right*) are usually grown for their colourful autumn foliage. Grow them over sheds and outbuildings, along perimeter walls or sturdy fences around the garden, or confine them to a trellis or pergola. Whichever approach you choose, a little pruning won't go amiss. If cutting in summer, remember that you may be sacrificing some autumn leaf colour.

How to prune For vines grown informally, trim back stems to keep the plant within bounds in midwinter and midsummer. For plants trained on a wall, pergola, or trellis, cut back the side shoots to between three and four buds of the main stems in late winter or early spring.

Make new plants by layering

Layering is a simple way of propagating plants by wounding a low-growing stem and keeping it in contact with the soil until roots form. This basic technique can be used for many climbers.

Some climbing plants, including the star jasmine (*Trachelospermum*) and ivy, will layer themselves when a stem or branch comes into contact with the soil. Most climbers, though, require a helping hand, either by simple layering or serpentine layering. Below is a list of climbers that can be propagated using these methods.

Simple layering
- *Akebia quinata*
- *Humulus lupulus*
- *Passiflora caerulea*
- *Pileostegia viburnoides*
- *Schizophragma integrifolium*
- *Vitis coignetiae*

Serpentine layering
- *Ampelopsis brevipedunculata*
- *Campsis x tagliabuana*
- *Celastrus orbiculatus*
- *Clematis*
- *Holboellia coriacea*

1 In spring, bury a 10cm (4in) pot, almost to its rim, in the soil close to the plant you want to layer. Fill it with fresh, multi-purpose compost and lightly firm with your fingers.

2 Take a healthy, low-growing stem and stretch it across the pot surface. With a sharp, clean knife make a nick in the underside of the stem, halfway between two sets of leaves.

3 Dip the exposed cut in some hormone rooting powder to help speed up the formation of roots. Remove any excess powder by gently tapping the stem with your fingers. Wash your hands after handling the rooting powder.

4 Bend a small piece of wire to form a "U" shape and place over the stem, pushing the cut below the surface of the compost. Cover with a little more compost if necessary.

5 Tie the free end of the stem to a cane support alongside the sunken pot. By autumn, roots should have formed. Then sever the layer close to the parent plant using secateurs, and cut the old stem on the layer back to the roots.

Serpentine layering

Serpentine layering allows more than one plant to be created from each stem. In spring, make a series of wounds between the leaf joints of the chosen stem and treat each with hormone rooting powder. Peg the cut sections of stem just below the soil surface with bent wire. Cover with extra soil if necessary. The young plants should be ready for separation from the parent plant in autumn.

Propagate new plants from cuttings

To make new plants, you can either take softwood cuttings from new shoot tips in spring, or firmer, semi-ripe cuttings later in the summer. The process for each is much the same, but softwood cuttings are less reliable.

Plants for propagating from semi-ripe cuttings

- *Akebia*
- *Berberidopsis*
- *Campsis*
- *Clematis*
- *Passiflora*
- *Trachelospermum*

Plants for propagating from softwood cuttings

- *Bignonia*
- *Hedera* (some)
- *Hydrangea*
- *Lonicera* (some)
- *Schisandra*
- *Wisteria*

1 For semi-ripe cuttings, cut 10–15cm (4–6in) lengths of stem with sharp secateurs – the stems should bend slightly when flexed – from midsummer to early autumn. Take 4–5cm (1½–2in) softwood cuttings in late spring.

2 Trim each cutting to just below a leaf joint, using a sharp, clean knife or secateurs. Remove the lowest leaves by pulling them off with your fingers to leave a clear length of stem. Cut the leaves of softwood cuttings in half.

3 Although most cuttings will root without any help, you can increase their chances by dipping the cut ends in hormone rooting powder. Tap the cutting to shake off any excess powder, and wash your hands afterwards.

4 Fill a pot with cuttings compost mixed with a little perlite for drainage. Insert the cuttings at equal spacings, but don't let the leaves touch each other. A 9cm (3½in) pot will hold around ten cuttings. Water well.

5 Cover the pot with a clear plastic bag, held above the cuttings with sticks and with an elastic band around the pot rim. Place in a propagator, or on a warm windowsill, until the cuttings have rooted, about 8–12 weeks later.

Caring for climbers

All plants need a little care and attention to perform well, and climbers are no exception. Making sure that they are well watered and receive the right amount of nutrients are basic maintenance tasks, while keeping your eyes peeled for signs of pests and diseases is also essential. In this chapter, find out how to water without wastage, and how and when to apply plant food to keep climbers healthy. Also, discover what pests and diseases are likely to attack your plants and how to minimize their effects. The seasonal plant care charts at the end of the chapter outline the jobs that need doing throughout the year.

Watering and feeding climbers

To get the most from your climbing plants, it is important to water and feed them regularly. Water is in increasingly short supply, so choose a watering method that will keep plants healthy while minimizing wastage.

What to water and when Mature plants will only need watering during prolonged hot spells, but young plants, those that have just been planted, and climbers in pots will need watering more regularly. Water early in the morning or in the evening when evaporation rates are lowest.

Wise ways to water There are many efficient watering methods, but splashing lots of water all over the flowers or leaves is not one of them because most will probably evaporate or run off before the plant roots have had a chance to absorb it. If you are watering by hand, direct the flow from your can or hose onto the soil around the base of the trunk or stem, to avoid wastage.

A watering system consisting of a network of porous hoses laid on the soil surface close to vulnerable plants' roots is an economical way of watering. Controlled manually or by a timer, which will switch the supply on and off at pre-programmed times, the leaky hoses drip water directly onto the soil. To increase efficiency further, cover the hosepipes with a mulch.

Watering climbers in containers Climbers grown in containers are more likely to suffer from a lack of water than those growing in a border, because the roots are confined to a set quantity of compost. In hot weather, pot-grown climbers may require watering more than once a day. When planting climbers, add some water-retaining gel to the compost to help conserve a little extra moisture. Check all of your plants daily and water when required, giving them a long drink each time to ensure water filters down to the bottom of the container. You could also consider investing in an automated watering system that will connect all of your pots and containers via a central timer. This allows you to set regular watering intervals even when you are out or on holiday.

Food for young plants To get your young climbing plants off to a good start, give them all the help you can. When planting, incorporate some well-rotted farmyard manure or garden compost in the planting hole and the surrounding soil. This organic matter will release nutrients slowly, helping young plants to develop strong, healthy growth. (It will also improve the water-holding properties of the soil.) Alternatively, mix a proprietary man-made general fertilizer with the soil used to backfill the planting hole. This comes in the form of small white granules, making it easy to see on the soil as you apply it. Follow the manufacturer's recommendations for application rates – young plants require a lower dose than mature plants.

Annual feeds You don't necessarily have to feed your plants according to a strict schedule of applications. Slow-release or controlled-release fertilizers can be added to the soil or compost just once each season and then left to release nutrients over a period of time at a carefully governed rate. The granules may be added at planting time or lightly forked into the soil around an established climber. The benefit of this type of feeding is that you only have to remember to do it once and are much less likely to inadvertently overfeed your plants, which can cause them more harm than underfeeding. As with all feeds, follow the manufacturer's instructions carefully.

Instant pick-me-ups Even if you have provided your climber with well-rotted manure and controlled-release fertilizer, it may still require a little boost of nutrients during the growing season. Your plants should only need this extra feed if you have very free-draining soil, where nutrients are washed out quickly, or if the leaves look yellow or discoloured, and you suspect a nutrient deficiency. Fast-acting feeds usually come in a liquid form, either ready-mixed or as a concentrate, or as a dissolvable powder to be mixed with water. Liquid feeds are generally applied to the soil using a watering can or, in some cases, to the foliage for rapid take-up of food. You can also buy a liquid feed concentrate in a canister, which attaches to your hosepipe; as you water the plants, a measured amount of fertilizer is automatically mixed with the water.

Keeping pests at bay

No matter how careful you are, pests are sure to appear at some point on at least one of your climbing plants.

Keep plants healthy to resist attacks, and if you see pests on your plants, take immediate action to minimize damage.

Resist attack Grow naturally resistant varieties of your favourite plants to reduce the chances of attack. Keep plants growing healthily, too, and choose those that grow well in the conditions in your garden. Vigorous, healthy plants are less likely to succumb to pests and diseases than weak, spindly ones.

Early warning signs Walk around your garden daily, if possible, to inspect plants for pest damage. At the first signs, identify the culprit and decide on the best course of action to combat it. If caught and treated early enough, many pests can be either eradicated altogether or at least kept at a manageable level.

Gardeners' friends Encourage ladybirds, lacewings, and other beneficial insects to take up residence in the garden. Left to their own devices, these environmentally friendly pest exterminators will soon prove their worth. Remember that many pesticides will also kill ladybirds and lacewings.

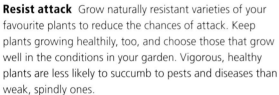
Ladybird larva

Eliminating problems Some simple methods of dealing with pests prove very effective, such as trapping earwigs in upturned flowerpots stuffed with hay or straw. Some pests, though, are most effectively dealt with using chemicals, and you should choose the product best suited to the job in hand and use it sparingly.

Identifying common pests

Whitefly Tiny sap-sucking insects that distort leaves and excrete a sugary substance on which sooty moulds grow. Control with proprietary spray.

Capsid bug Adult capsid bugs suck the sap from plant shoots, causing distorted and holey leaves. Control with proprietary spray.

Vine weevils Adult weevils eat leaf margins, while their grubs eat roots, causing stems to die. Drench soil with proprietary insecticide or nematodes.

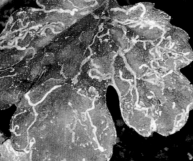

Slugs and snails In damp weather and at night, slugs and snails come out to eat leaves, stems, and fruits. Use slug pellets or organic controls.

Leaf miner The larvae of these insects create pale-coloured "tunnels". Pick off and destroy leaves as soon as they are seen.

Red spider mite Leaf mottling and very fine webbing on young shoots and leaves are signs of red spider mite. Use biological control or spray.

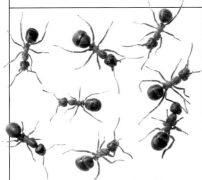

Ants Ants create nests that disturb roots and defend aphids so they can feed off their honeydew. They are more of a nuisance than a pest to plants.

Aphids These sap-sucking pests cause distorted growth. Encourage ladybirds and lacewings to feed on them, or use a spray.

Earwigs Chewed flower petals may be due to earwigs. Catch them using upturned pots filled with hay or straw (*see p.116*) or spray with insecticide.

Preventing diseases

When tackling plant diseases, prevention is better than cure, so check plants regularly for any early warning signs. If your plants do look sickly, identify the problem and treat it promptly.

Give plants what they need
The best way to prevent disease is to keep your plants healthy, because strong plants are more able to fight off a disease attack than weak ones. Plant them in the right conditions, bearing in mind their hardiness, preferred soil type, drainage needs, aspect, and feeding requirements.

Virus alert Viruses commonly show themselves as distorted or stunted growth, and white-streaked or discoloured flowers and leaves. Remove any virused plants promptly, wash your tools, and don't replant the area with a similar type of plant.

Preventing problems Stop diseases spreading by keeping the ground around your plants clear of plant debris. Remove and dispose of fallen leaves, dying stems, dead flowers, and any growth that looks diseased. Do this as often as you are can.

Cures for diseases Diseases often need treating with a specially formulated spray. Before buying a product, make sure you have correctly identified the problem by checking books or websites, or by consulting a gardening expert.

Identifying common diseases

Clematis wilt Leaves and shoots wilt and then die. Prune out infected wood. By planting clematis deeper than when in its original pot, there is a chance that protected dormant buds below the soil surface will reshoot when clematis wilt strikes.

Coral spot Look out for tiny orange pustules on dead, woody stems and branches. This fungus can spread from dead wood to healthy tissue and kill the plant. Prune out and dispose of any infected wood, and do not compost the clippings.

Downy mildew Discoloured areas appear on leaves and a grey fuzz develops on the undersides. Remove and dispose of infected leaves, and increase air flow around plants. Avoid overhead watering.

Powdery mildew A white powder covers the leaves and shoots of affected plants. Remove and dispose of infected parts. Avoid overhead watering, especially if plants are growing in dry soils. If necessary, spray with an appropriate fungicide.

Rust Usually orange or brown pustules appear on leaves and stems. Remove offending parts of the plant and dispose of them. Increase air circulation around plants and spray with a fungicide if necessary. Try growing rust-resistant varieties.

Black spot This fungal disease causes black spots on rose leaves, which eventually fall. Prune out affected leaves and dispose of them. Spray in spring with an approved fungicide, and repeat-spray following the manufacturer's instructions.

Plant guide

The following plants include some of the most beautiful climbers for your garden. To help you make your selection, they are set out in the following groups: clematis, climbers, and roses. Many have the RHS Award of Garden Merit, which means that they are excellent plants for garden use.

Key to plant symbols

☘   Plants given the RHS Award of Garden Merit

Soil preference

♢   Well-drained soil

♢   Moist soil

♦   Wet soil

Preference for sun or shade

☀   Full sun

◑   Partial or dappled shade

☀   Full shade

Hardiness ratings

✳✳✳   Fully hardy plants

✳✳   Plants that survive outside in mild regions or sheltered sites

✳   Plants that need protection from frost over winter

❂   Tender plants that do not tolerate any degree of frost

Clematis (Ab–Di)

Clematis 'Abundance'

This viticella-type clematis produces small, pinkish-red flowers from midsummer to late autumn. Each bloom has four spaced sepals and cream anthers. Ideal for growing through shrubs. Prune all stems down to the soil in spring.

H: 3m (10ft), Group 3
❄❄❄ ◊ ◗ ☼ ◑ ♚

Clematis 'Alba Luxurians'

A viticella-type clematis with grey-green foliage and small, white flowers with green-tipped sepals that blooms from midsummer to late autumn. It is best grown through trees and shrubs. Prune all stems down to the soil in spring.

H: 4m (12ft), Group 3
❄❄❄ ◊ ◗ ☼ ◑ ♚

Clematis alpina 'Willy'

Also known as C. 'Willy', this clematis flowers from spring to early summer. Its small, light pink blooms are darker on the underside and towards the base, and have clusters of cream anthers. Fluffy seedheads follow the flowers. Prune thinly, if required.

H: 2–3m (6–10ft), Group 1
❄❄❄ ◊ ◗ ☼ ◑

Clematis 'Arabella'

This non-clinging clematis with small, violet-blue flowers in mid- to late summer is perfect for scrambling through a mixed border or trained up an arch. Prune the previous season's growth to just above the soil in early spring.

H: 2m (6ft), Group 3
❄❄ ◊ ◗ ☼ ♚

Clematis armandii

There is little to match this vigorous evergreen for its mass of small, white, scented flowers produced in early spring. This plant will climb through trees and quickly cover sheds and walls. No pruning is necessary but it can be lightly pruned to keep in check.

H: 3–5m (10–15ft), Group 1
❄❄ ◊ ◗ ☼ ◑

Clematis 'Barbara Jackman'

This summer-flowering, deciduous hybrid has large, single, blue-mauve blooms with a darker central stripe, but the colour can fade in bright sun. The mid-green foliage comprises three leaflets. Prune lightly in late winter or early spring.

H: 2.5–3m (8–10ft), Group 2
❄❄❄ ◊ ◗ ☼ ◑

Clematis 'Bees' Jubilee'

A deciduous, compact hybrid that is ideal for containers. It has large, single, mid-pink flowers with a dark pink central band on each sepal, borne in late spring and early summer. The flower colour fades with age. Prune lightly in late winter or early spring.

H: 2.5m (8ft), Group 2
❄❄❄ ◊ ◑ ☼ ☀

Clematis 'Bill MacKenzie'

This vigorous clematis produces small, single, bright yellow, bell-shaped flowers with thick, almost waxy, sepals from midsummer to late autumn. Large, fluffy seedheads follow. Prune all stems down to soil level in early spring.

H: 7m (22ft), Group 3
❄❄❄ ◊ ◑ ☼ ☀ ☼ ♧

Clematis 'Blue Ravine'

A large-flowered hybrid that has wavy-edged, soft violet sepals with a darker midrib. The plant flowers mainly in late spring and early summer, with a further flush of blooms in late summer. Prune lightly in late winter or early spring.

H: 2.5–3m (8–10ft), Group 2
❄❄❄ ◊ ◑ ☼ ☀

Clematis cirrhosa

Glossy, evergreen leaves and cream, bell-shaped blooms in late winter and early spring are a cheerful sight. The leaves of *C. cirrhosa* 'Wisley Cream' are bronze, while the flowers of *C. cirrhosa* 'Freckles' are blotched purple inside. Prune lightly, if necessary.

H: 2.5–3m (8–10ft), Group 1
❄❄ ◊ ◑ ☼ ☀

Clematis 'Comtesse de Bouchaud'

This reliable old variety produces small, single, soft pink flowers in summer. They have distinctive sepals that bend back slightly at the tips, accentuating the yellow anthers. Prune all stems down to soil level in early spring.

H: 2–3m (6–10ft), Group 3
❄❄❄ ◊ ◑ ☼ ☀ ♧

Clematis x diversifolia

Small, bell-shaped, indigo-violet flowers with creamy-yellow anthers are produced in summer and autumn. Grow through shrubs or into small trees to support the non-clinging stems. Prune all stems down to soil level in early spring.

H: 2.5m (8ft), Group 3
❄❄❄ ◊ ◑ ☼ ☀

Clematis (Do–He)

Clematis '*Doctor Ruppel*'
This deciduous, large-flowered clematis blooms all summer and looks particularly striking over a pergola or around a front door. Its rich pink flowers have a darker middle stripe and an eye of brown anthers. Prune lightly in late winter or early spring.

H: 2.5m (8ft), Group 2
❄❄❄ ◊ ◖ ☼ ◐ ♈

Clematis '*Duchess of Albany*'
From midsummer to autumn, this deciduous texensis-type clematis produces small, rich pink flowers with a dark pink stripe. Show off the flowers by planting it with evergreen shrubs such as yew. Prune all stems down to the soil in early spring.

H: 2.5m (8ft), Group 3
❄❄❄ ◊ ◖ ☼ ◐

Clematis '*Duchess of Edinburgh*'
This double-flowered hybrid produces pure white blooms with yellow anthers in early summer. The first flowers of the season may be green-tinged, with those at the end single rather than double. Prune lightly in late winter or early spring.

H: 2.5m (8ft), Group 2
❄❄❄ ◊ ◖ ☼ ◐

Clematis *x durandii*
A loosely climbing hybrid, dating back to 1870, that produces small, single, indigo-blue flowers with a central boss of golden-yellow anthers in late summer. Its deciduous leaves are glossy green. Prune all stems down to the soil in early spring.

H: 1–2m (3–6ft), Group 3
❄❄ ◊ ◖ ☼ ◐ ♈

Clematis '*Elizabeth*'
This vigorous, montana-type clematis will quickly cover a support. It produces a profusion of small, pale pink, scented flowers in late spring and early summer. Its deciduous foliage is flushed purple. Prune lightly, if required.

H: 7m (22ft), Group 1
❄❄❄ ◊ ◖ ☼ ◐ ♈

Clematis '*Etoile Violette*'
A viticella-type clematis producing an abundance of small, deep violet flowers with yellow anthers from midsummer to late autumn. Plant with pale-leaved or pale-flowered shrubs to accentuate the blooms. Prune all stems down to the soil in early spring.

H: 3–5m (10–15ft), Group 3
❄❄❄ ◊ ◖ ☼ ◐ ♈

Clematis '*Fireworks*'

A vibrant-coloured hybrid that has long-lasting, large magenta flowers, with a darker central stripe. It blooms from late spring to early summer, and is ideal for a patio container, where it can be easily admired. Prune lightly in late winter or early spring.

H: 3m (10ft), Group 2
❄❄❄ ◊ ◊ ☼

Clematis florida *var.* sieboldiana

This deciduous or semi-evergreen climber has distinctive, pure white flowers with a large boss of purple stamens in late spring or summer. It can be grown in a container in a warm, sheltered spot. Prune lightly in late winter or early spring.

H: 2–2.5m (6–8ft), Group 2
❄❄ ◊ ◊ ☼ ☼

Clematis '*Frances Rivis*'

An alpina-type clematis that bears slate-blue, nodding, bell-shaped flowers with white centres in late spring. It looks particularly attractive if allowed to spill over a wall or fence. The spent blooms develop into fluffy seedheads. Prune lightly, if required.

H: 2–3m (6–10ft), Group 1
❄❄❄ ◊ ◊ ☼ ☼ ❧

Clematis '*Gillian Blades*'

From late spring to early summer, this climber produces large, pure white, single flowers with wavy margins and cream anthers. It has deciduous mid-green leaves. Water well for a good display. Prune lightly in late winter or early spring.

H: 2.5m (8ft), Group 2
❄❄❄ ◊ ◊ ☼ ☼ ❧

Clematis '*Guernsey Cream*'

One of the first large-flowered hybrids to bloom, this clematis produces single, cream flowers with creamy-yellow anthers in early summer. Grow in dappled shade to prevent the flower colour from fading. Prune lightly in late winter or early spring.

H: 2.5m (8ft), Group 2
❄❄❄ ◊ ◊ ☼ ☼

Clematis '*Helsingborg*'

In late spring, this alpina-type clematis bears blue-purple, nodding, bell-shaped flowers. It can be grown in a large pot. In late summer and autumn, the fluffy seedheads are a feature. No pruning is necessary but the plant can be thinned.

H: 2–3m (6–10ft), Group 1
❄❄❄ ◊ ◊ ☼ ☼ ❧

Clematis (He–Ma)

Clematis 'Henryi'

This summer-flowering hybrid has the largest blooms – up to 20cm (8in) across – of all clematis. The flowers are pure white with a centre of brown anthers on white stamens. It makes an ideal container plant. Prune lightly in late winter or early spring.

H: 3m (10ft), Group 2
✽✽✽ ○ ◐ ☼ ◑ ♚

Clematis heracleifolia 'Wyevale'

A woody-based, herbaceous clematis with small, tubular, bright blue flowers in summer. Sometimes classified as *C. tubulosa* 'Wyevale', this plant can be used as ground cover or supported to reach its full height. Prune all stems down to soil level in early spring.

H: 75cm (30in), Group 3
✽✽✽ ○ ◐ ☼ ◑ ♚

Clematis 'H.F. Young'

This compact, deciduous, glossy-leaved clematis bears large, single, blue flowers with a cream eye in early summer. Grow on trellis around a doorway or on wires against a warm wall. Prune lightly in late winter or early spring.

H: 2.5m (8ft), Group 2
✽✽✽ ○ ◐ ☼ ◑

Clematis 'Huldine'

This is a particularly strong-growing, deciduous clematis, ideal for walls and fences. In summer, it bears a profusion of small white flowers, with purple stripes on the reverse. Grow over walls and fences. Prune all stems to soil level in early spring.

H: 3–5m (10–15ft), Group 3
✽✽✽ ○ ◐ ☼ ◑ ♚

Clematis 'Imperial'

An easy, large-flowered clematis that will clothe pergolas and pyramids when grown in a border or container. Single, occasionally double, creamy-pink blooms with a darker central stripe appear in early summer. Prune lightly in late winter or early spring.

H: 2.5–3m (8–10ft), Group 2
✽✽✽ ○ ◐ ☼ ◑

Clematis integrifolia

This non-twining herbaceous clematis scrambles up through other plants for support. In summer, it bears small, violet-blue, bell-shaped flowers with twisted sepals. These develop into silver-brown seedheads. Prune stems down to soil level in early spring.

H: 60cm (24in), Group 3
✽✽✽ ○ ◐ ☼ ◑

Clematis 'Jackmanii'

This vigorous, large-flowered clematis is best grown around doorways and windows, where its abundance of striking flowers can be appreciated. Single, dark purple blooms appear from mid- to late summer. Prune all stems down to the soil in early spring.

H: 3m (10ft), Group 3
❄❄❄ ○ ◐ ☼ ☀ ♈

Clematis *Josephine*

A consistently double variety with rosette-like, mauve-pink flowers from mid- to late summer. It needs full sun for strong flower colour; in the shade, blooms take on a greenish hue. A good choice for containers. Prune lightly in late winter or early spring.

H: 2.5m (8ft), Group 2
❄❄❄ ○ ◐ ☼ ♈

Clematis koreana

This deciduous clematis produces purple, nodding flowers, which turn yellow inside and at the margins, in late spring and early summer. *C. koreana* var. *lutea* has purer yellow flowers. No pruning is necessary but the plant can be thinned.

H: 4m (12ft), Group 1
❄❄❄ ○ ◐ ☼ ☀

Clematis 'Lady Londesborough'

The large, pink-mauve, fading to silver-mauve, flowers of this clematis are best appreciated against darker-leaved plants. The blooms appear from late spring to early summer and again in late summer. Prune lightly in late winter or early spring.

H: 2m (6ft), Group 2
❄❄❄ ○ ◐ ☼ ☀

Clematis 'Lasurstern'

This is a very free-flowering, deciduous clematis with large, blue-purple blooms in early summer, and a reduced flush later on. It produces its best flower colour when grown in partial shade. Prune lightly in late winter or early spring.

H: 2.5 (8ft), Group 2
❄❄❄ ○ ◐ ☼ ☀ ♈

Clematis macropetala

A deciduous climber that bears from spring to early summer small, open, bell-shaped, violet-blue flowers that give the impression of being double. Silver seedheads follow later in the year, extending the season of interest. Thin out crowded stems, if required.

H: 2–3m (6–10ft), Group 1
❄❄❄ ○ ◐ ☼ ☀

Clematis (Ma–Om)

Clematis 'Madame Julia Correvon'
This viticella-type clematis produces small, wine-red flowers over a long period from midsummer until late autumn. With their twisted sepals, the blooms look like tiny propellers. Prune all stems down to the ground in early spring.

H: 3m (10ft), Group 3
✿✿✿ ○ ◑ ☼ ☀ ♉

Clematis 'Marie Boisselot'
From midsummer to late autumn, this reliable climber flowers bears large, single, pure white flowers with a ridged line in the centre of each sepal. It is a good choice for covering an arbour or wrought-iron fence. Prune lightly in late winter or early spring.

H: 3m (10ft), Group 2
✿✿✿ ○ ◑ ☼ ☀ ♉

Clematis 'Markham's Pink'
A vigorous and prolific macropetala-type clematis that produces masses of bright pink, double flowers from spring to early summer. It is a delightful clematis, best grown up a trellis or through shrubs and small trees. Thin out stems, if required.

H: 2–3m (6–10ft), Group 1
✿✿✿ ○ ◑ ☼ ☀ ♉

Clematis 'Minuet'
This distinctive, small-flowered climber bears single, white flowers with pinkish-purple veins and sepal tips from midsummer until late autumn. It makes a striking partner for shrubs and small trees. Prune all stems down to the soil in early spring.

H: 3m (10ft), Group 3
✿✿✿ ○ ◑ ☼ ☀ ♉

Clematis 'Miss Bateman'
Large, single, white flowers with red anthers and a creamy-yellow stripe in the centre of each sepal are borne in early summer. The blooms are striking against the deciduous foliage. Grow in a container or against trellis. Prune lightly in late winter or early spring.

H: 2.5m (8ft), Group 2
✿✿✿ ○ ◑ ☼ ☀ ♉

Clematis montana *var.* grandiflora
This very vigorous grower, which will quickly cover its support, produces a profusion of large, white flowers in late spring and early summer. It has dark green deciduous foliage. No pruning is necessary but the plant can be thinned, if required.

H: 10m (30ft), Group 1
✿✿✿ ○ ◑ ☼ ☀ ♉

Clematis montana *var.* rubens
In late spring and early summer, this extremely vigorous clematis bears masses of pink flowers with cream anthers at the centre. It has bronze-green, deciduous foliage. Use it to screen an outbuilding or clamber up a tree. Thin out stems, if required.

H: 5m (15ft), Group 1
❋❋❋ ◊ ◖ ☼ ☀

Clematis montana *var.* rubens 'Tetrarose'
A very vigorous, deciduous clematis that flowers in late spring and early summer. It has purple-green leaves and small, pink flowers with cream anthers. No pruning is necessary but the plant can be thinned.

H: 10m (30ft), Group 1
❋❋❋ ◊ ◖ ☼ ☀

Clematis '*Mrs George Jackman*'
In early summer, this deciduous climber produces large, semi-double, creamy-white blooms, with a cream stripe on each sepal. Try growing it in a container with a tall support such as a metal obelisk. Prune lightly in late winter or early spring.

H: 2.5m (8ft), Group 2
❋❋❋ ◊ ◖ ☼ ☀ ♥

Clematis '*Nelly Moser*'
In early summer, this clematis displays large, single, white blooms, suffused pink, with a darker pink central stripe on each sepal. A spray of red anthers adds to the show. Plant in the shade to prevent blooms fading. Prune lightly in late winter or early spring.

H: 2–3m (6–10ft), Group 2
❋❋❋ ◊ ◖ ☼ ♥

Clematis '*Niobe*'
From late spring until autumn, this compact clematis bears large, single, deep red blooms with yellow anthers. Grow it in a container, around a porch, or let it wander through a shrub border. Prune lightly in late winter or early spring.

H: 2–3m (6–10ft), Group 2
❋❋❋ ◊ ◖ ☼ ☀ ♥

Clematis '*Omoshiro*'
This most striking clematis has large, pink-white flowers with purple-pink margins in early summer, and another flush of blooms in late summer. It looks particularly effective against a darker backdrop. Prune lightly in late winter or early spring.

H: 2–2.5m (6–8ft), Group 2
❋❋❋ ◊ ◖ ☼ ☀

Clematis (Pe–Ro)

Clematis '*Perle d'Azur*'
Popular for its freely borne, small, blue-purple flowers, this vigorous clematis produces a profusion of blooms from midsummer to autumn. The sepal tips curl back and the anthers are cream-coloured. Prune all stems down to the soil in early spring.

H: 3m (10ft), Group 3
❀❀❀ ◊ ◊ ☼ ☼

Clematis '*Plum Beauty*'
This clematis is a good choice for a patio container. Its reddish-purple, nodding, bell-shaped flowers with mauve margins appear in mid- to late spring. The flowers are followed by attractive yellow seedheads. Prune thinly, if required.

H: 3m (10ft), Group 1
❀❀❀ ◊ ◊ ☼ ☼

Clematis '*Polish Spirit*'
A vigorous clematis with small, single, velvet-maroon blooms from midsummer until late autumn. It can be trained to grow through trees and shrubs to add some late season splashes of colour. Prune all stems down to the soil in early spring.

H: 5m (15ft), Group 3
❀❀❀ ◊ ◊ ☼ ☼ ♀

Clematis '*Prince Charles*'
Ideal for small gardens, this climber bears large, bluish-purple flowers with clusters of yellow stamens from midsummer to autumn. Flower colour may vary according to whether it is grown in sun or shade. Prune all stems down to the soil in early spring.

H: 2–2.5m (6–8ft), Group 3
❀❀❀ ◊ ◊ ☼ ☼ ♀

Clematis '*Princess Alexandra*'
This striking deciduous climber has large double and semi-double, pink flowers with paler central stripes and a cluster of yellow stamens. It flowers in early summer and again in late summer with single blooms only. Prune lightly in late winter or early spring.

H: 2–2.5m (6–8ft), Group 2
❀❀ ◊ ◊ ☼ ☼

Clematis '*Purpurea Plena Elegans*'
The profusion of double, purple-mauve blooms, up to 8cm (3in) across, provide an effective foil for the pale green, deciduous foliage. The flowers appear from midsummer until late autumn. Prune all stems down to the soil in early spring.

H: 3m (10ft), Group 3
❀❀❀ ◊ ◊ ☼ ☼ ♀

Clematis recta
This climber attracts butterflies and hoverflies. Its tiny, star-shaped, strongly perfumed white flowers appear from midsummer to autumn. A few canes or nearby plants will help to keep it upright. Prune all stems down to the soil in early spring.

H: 1–2m (3–6ft), Group 3
❁❁❁ ◊ ◗ ☼ ☀

Clematis rehderiana
Nodding, creamy-yellow bells with a cowslip scent are the hallmark of this vigorous species. Clusters of blooms are held aloft from the mid-green, vine-like leaves from midsummer until late autumn. Prune all stems down to the soil in early spring.

H: 6–7m (20–22ft), Group 3
❁❁❁ ◊ ◗ ☼ ☀ ♀

Clematis 'Richard Pennell'
A large-flowered clematis bearing in early summer single, deep-purple blooms with yellow anthers and a slightly crinkled appearance. Grow against a trellis or an arbour for a vibrant display. Prune lightly in late winter or early spring.

H: 2–3m (6–10ft), Group 2
❁❁❁ ◊ ◗ ☼ ☀ ♀

Clematis 'Rosy O'Grady'
This alpina-type clematis bears semi-double, mauve-pink, open, bell-shaped flowers in spring and again in summer until autumn. Train up a pillar in the border or on a pyramid in a container to give the flowers ample space. Prune thinly, if required.

H: 2.5–5m (8–15ft), Group 1
❁❁❁ ◊ ◗ ☼ ♀

Clematis 'Rosy Pagoda'
An alpina-type clematis with open, bell-shaped, pink flowers with full creamy-white centres in mid- to late spring. Fluffy seedheads provide autumn interest. Encourage it to scramble up small trees or through shrubs. Prune lightly, if required.

H: 2.5–5m (8–15ft), Group 1
❁❁❁ ◊ ◗ ☼

Clematis 'Rouge Cardinal'
A large-flowered variety producing sumptuous, single, crimson blooms with reddish-brown anthers in midsummer. To really perform well, it needs a sunny site and support, such as a trellis or pergola. Prune all stems down to the soil in early spring.

H: 2–3m (6–10ft), Group 3
❁❁❁ ◊ ◗ ☼

Clematis (Ro–Wi)

Clematis 'Royalty'
In early summer, this compact clematis bears large, semi-double, mauve-purple blooms with a central boss of yellow anthers. A second flush in late summer produces smaller, single flowers. Prune lightly in late winter or early spring.

H: 2m (6ft), Group 2
❅❅❅ ◊ ◊ ☼ ☼ ♈

Clematis 'Rüütel'
Large, deep purple-red blooms up to 20cm (8in) across, with a darker central band, are produced in summer. A cluster of reddish-brown anthers sits at the centre of each flower. Prune lightly in late winter or early spring.

H: 3m (10ft), Group 2
❅❅❅ ◊ ◊ ☼ ☼

Clematis tangutica
This very vigorous species produces bell-shaped, pure yellow flowers from midsummer until late autumn. Fluffy seedheads follow the flowers – often both are on show at the same time. Prune all stems down to the soil in early spring.

H: 5–6m (15–20ft), Group 3
❅❅❅ ◊ ◊ ☼ ☼

Clematis 'The President'
This is an old variety bearing large, single, blue-purple flowers with red anthers. It flowers profusely throughout summer and is often grown on trellis, against walls, and in containers. Prune lightly in late winter or early spring.

H: 2–3m (6–10ft), Group 2
❅❅❅ ◊ ◊ ☼ ☼ ♈

Clematis x triternata 'Rubromarginata'
A vigorous clematis producing small, star-like blooms with a cluster of yellow stamens from summer until autumn. The red-purple sepals fade to white at the base. Prune all stems down to the soil in early spring.

H: 3–6m (10–20ft), Group 3
❅❅❅ ◊ ◊ ☼ ☼ ♈

Clematis 'Venosa Violacea'
Small, single, purple flowers with white bands tapering to the ends of the sepals and a dark central eye appear on this viticella-type clematis from midsummer until late autumn. Prune all stems down to the soil in early spring.

H: 3m (10ft), Group 3
❅❅❅ ◊ ◊ ☼ ☼ ♈

Clematis 'Veronica's Choice'
Large, very pale mauve, almost white, semi-double blooms are borne in early summer. In the centre of each flower is a cluster of cream anthers. A second flush in late summer produces only single blooms. Prune lightly in late winter or early spring.

H: 2.5m (8ft), Group 2
❀❀❀ ◊ ◑ ☼ ☀

Clematis 'Ville de Lyon'
This clematis produces large, maroon, single flowers in midsummer. It tends to have quite sparse foliage towards the base so it is a good idea to grow it with, or through, other plants to mask the bare stems. Prune all stems down the soil in early spring.

H: 2–3m (6–10ft), Group 3
❀❀❀ ◊ ◑ ☼ ☀

Clematis 'Vyvyan Pennell'
An ideal clematis to grow in a container, or up a trellis, pyramid, or pillar. It has attractive, large, double, lilac flowers in midsummer; later in the season the flowers are bluer. The deciduous foliage is mid-green. Prune lightly in late winter or early spring.

H: 2–3m (6–10ft), Group 2
❀❀❀ ◊ ◑ ☼ ☀

Clematis 'W.E. Gladstone'
This variety has huge purple blooms that, with their overlapping sepals, look circular; they have a central eye of dark red anthers. Position the plant where its flowers can be appreciated and provide sturdy support. Prune lightly in late winter or early spring.

H: 3m (10ft), Group 2
❀❀❀ ◊ ◑ ☼ ☀

Clematis 'White Swan'
A compact macropetala-type clematis that bears double, bell-shaped, white flowers with pale green-yellow centres in spring and early summer. It may repeat flower later. Grow dark-leaved plants nearby to accentuate the flowers. Prune thinly, if required.

H: 5m (15ft), Group 1
❀❀❀ ◊ ◑ ☼ ☀

Clematis 'William Kennett'
Large, dark purple-blue, single flowers with maroon anthers are borne in early summer. Central stripes on the sepals fade with age. Grow this vigorous climber in a border where it can scramble through shrubs. Prune lightly in late winter or early spring.

H: 2–3m (6–10ft), Group 2
❀❀❀ ◊ ◑ ☼ ☀

Climbers (Ac–Co)

Actinidia deliciosa

This vigorous, deciduous climber, also known as Kiwi fruit or Chinese gooseberry, is usually grown for its rounded leaves and red-tinged, hairy stems. In warmer climes, female plants produce fruits. Creamy-white flowers in early summer gradually turn yellow.

H: 10m (30ft)

❄❄ ◊ ☼ ☀

Actinidia kolomikta

A deciduous, twining climber that produces masses of purple-hued young leaves, turning dark green with a distinct pink and white variegation. In early summer, it bears clusters of small, lightly fragrant flowers. Train the stems along wires against a wall.

H: 5m (15ft) or more

❄❄❄ ◊ ☼ ♈

Akebia quinata

The chocolate vine has strong, twining stems and is semi-evergreen, retaining its foliage only in warm regions or mild winters. In spring, the mid-green leaves are accompanied by purple female flowers and smaller male blooms with a spicy fragrance.

H: 10m (30ft)

❄❄❄ ◊ ◊ ☼ ☀

Akebia trifoliata

A deciduous, twining climber that, given a strong trellis against a sunny or partially shady wall, will repay you with a lush screen of foliage from spring to autumn. In spring, pendent, purple flowers appear as the young, bronzy leaves mature to a rich green.

H: 10m (30ft)

❄❄❄ ◊ ◊ ☼ ☀ ♈

Ampelopsis brevipedunculata

A vigorous climber with three-lobed, hop-like, mid-green leaves. Its summer flowers are green, and largely inconspicuous, but they are followed by beautiful porcelain-blue berries in early autumn. Prune, if needed, in late winter or early spring.

H: 5m (15ft)

❄❄❄ ◊ ◊ ☼ ☀

Berberidopsis corralina

An evergreen climber from Chile with attractive foliage and flowers. Its rounded leaves with spiny edges are rich green above and white below. In mid- to late summer, necklace-like stems of red flowers, resembling tiny berries, are produced. Provide support.

H: 5m (15ft)

❄❄ ◊ ☀

Billardiera longiflora
An evergreen climber that produces dainty, greenish yellow, pendent flowers in summer. These are followed by glossy berries, usually purple-blue but also red, pink or white. In colder areas, this plant is best grown in a conservatory.

H: up to 3m (10ft)
❄❄ ◊ ☼ ◐ ❦ ♈

Campsis x tagliabuana
The trumpet vine is a vigorous, deciduous climber. On *C. x tagliabuana* 'Madame Galen' ♈, rich green divided leaves are bolstered in late summer by orange-red trumpet flowers. Grow against a sunny wall on sturdy horizontal wires.

H: 10m (30ft)
❄❄ ◑ ◊ ☼

Celastrus orbiculatus
A deciduous shrub that climbs by means of its woody stems. Its rounded, toothed, mid-green leaves turn a rich golden yellow in autumn. In summer, small green flowers give way to tiny yellow fruits that open to reveal bright reddish-pink seeds.

H: 14m (46ft)
❄❄❄ ◊ ☼ ◐

Celastrus scandens
A vigorous, deciduous shrub with rounded, mid-green leaves that turn golden in autumn. Tiny yellow-green summer flowers produce yellow fruits with scarlet seeds inside. Grow through a large tree, train against a wall, or let it cascade over a pergola.

H: 10m (30ft)
❄❄❄ ◊ ☼ ◐

Cobaea scandens
The cup and saucer vine is an evergreen perennial that is usually grown as an annual. Its large, fragrant, bell-shaped flowers with their distinctive "saucers" open a creamy-green before turning purple, and are enhanced by the dense foliage.

H: 10–20m (30–70ft)
❄ ◊ ◐ ♈

Codonopsis convolvulacea
This perennial climber has twining stems adorned with bluish-violet, occasionally white, bell-shaped flowers in summer. Provide twiggy support and a sheltered site to protect the brittle stems. To overwinter plants in cold areas, apply a thick mulch.

H: 2m (6ft)
❄❄❄ ◊ ☼ ◐

Climbers (Di–Ip)

Dicentra scandens
An annual climber bearing trumpet-shaped flowers throughout summer. Provide a bamboo wigwam, metal obelisk, or trellis for plants to climb up. Sow seed in spring for a summer display or sow in late summer for an earlier display the following year.

H: 2.5m (8ft)
❋ ❋ ❋ ◊ ☼

Eccremocarpus scaber
An evergreen, perennial, fast-growing climber that is perfect for clothing obelisks and wall-mounted trellises. Its divided leaves have an almost fern-like appearance. Orange-red tubular flowers cover the plant from late spring until autumn.

H: 3–5m (10–15ft)
❋ ❋ ◊ ☼

Fallopia baldschuanica
Also called mile-a-minute after its rampant nature, this very vigorous, twining, deciduous climber needs a strong support. Its woody stems are clothed with heart-shaped, dark green leaves and tiny, pink-tinged white flowers from summer to autumn.

H: 12m (40ft)
❋ ❋ ❋ ◊ ☼ ☼

Ficus pumila
This tender evergreen has tiny, rounded, dark green leaves. Self-clinging aerial roots mean that it needs no extra support. In cold areas, bring indoors in winter to protect from frost. *F. pumila* 'Variegata' has white-margined leaves.

H: 3–5m (10–15ft) or more
❀ ◊ ◊ ☼ ☼ ♆

Hardenbergia violacea
A vigorous climber with leathery, rich-green leaves and clusters of violet pea-like flowers from late winter to early summer. It is best grown as a short-lived perennial. Grow outdoors in a sunny position. In cold areas, grow in a greenhouse.

H: 2m (6ft) or more
❋ ◊ ☼ ☼ ♆

Hedera canariensis '*Ravensholst*'
Originating in North Africa, this vigorous, woody, evergreen climber has almost triangular, glossy green leaves up to 14cm (5½in) long. It climbs by clinging on with its aerial roots. Grow up an outside wall or over an old tree stump.

H: 5m (15ft)
❋ ❋ ◊ ☼ ☼ ♆

Hedera helix 'Glacier'
This woody, self-clinging, evergreen climber has small, triangular leaves marked with silver-grey and cream variegations. Its foliage will clothe a wall or the side of a shed to provide all-year interest, or it will turn an old tree trunk into a silvery centrepiece.

H: 10m (30ft)
❋❋❋ ◊ ☼ ☼ ☼ ♈

Hedera hibernica
The Irish ivy is a vigorous woody climber with glossy green, triangular leaves. Once at the top of its support, non-clinging stems are formed with clusters of unlobed leaves. Flowers and black fruit follow. Grow against a sunny wall or an old tree trunk.

H: 10m (30ft)
❋❋❋ ◊ ☼ ☼ ☼ ♈

Holboellia coriacea
A vigorous, evergreen, twining climber from China with dark green leaves and pale-coloured flowers, flushed purple-mauve. After a very warm summer, the flowers may give way to sausage-shaped fruits. Train on horizontal wires against a wall.

H: 7m (22ft)
❋❋ ◊ ☼ ☼

Humulus lupulus
The hop is a herbaceous perennial climber with bristly, twining stems. Its light green leaves are deeply lobed with toothed edges. *H. lupulus* 'Aureus' ♈ has golden yellow foliage. In summer, its flowers, or cones, ripen to a straw colour.

H: 6m (20ft)
❋❋❋ ◐ ◊ ☼ ☼

Hydrangea anomala *subsp.* **petiolaris**
This is a vigorous woody climber with broad, rounded, mid-green leaves and large, open heads of creamy-white flowers in summer. Young plants need support to establish themselves.

H: 15m (50ft)
❋❋❋ ◐ ◊ ☼ ☼ ♈

Ipomoea
Morning glory provides a feast of summer colour. *I. tricolor* 'Heavenly Blue' has blue trumpet-shaped flowers, *I. purpurea* offers purple, magenta, pink, white, or striped, *I. lobata* has tubular flowers that open red, fading to white. Grow from seed each year.

H: 3–5m (10–15ft)
❀ ◊ ☼

Climbers (Ja–Pa)

Jasminum officinale

The common jasmine has attractive fern-like foliage and star-like, strongly scented, white flowers. In cold winters, plants may die back but will reshoot from ground level in spring. 'Argenteovariegatum' ♥ has variegated foliage.

H: 12m (40ft)

❄❄ ◊ ☼ ◐ ♥

Lapageria rosea

The Chilean bellflower is a twining, evergreen climber that flowers from summer to late autumn. Pink-red, wax-like, trumpet-shaped blooms are produced singly, in twos or threes, and have slightly flared mouths. They nestle among the dark green foliage.

H: 5m (15ft)

❄❄ ◊ ◑ ☼ ♥

Lathyrus grandiflorus

The everlasting sweet pea is a perennial with mid-green leaves and racemes of pink-purple and red flowers in summer (these are less perfumed than those of *L. odoratus*). Its tendrils will take hold of any support, such as canes or trellis.

H: 1.5m (5ft)

❄❄❄ ◊ ☼ ◐

Lathyrus latifolius

In summer, this perennial sweet pea carries up to 11 pink-purple flowers on each flower stem. Its leaves are blue-green. The stems need support to reach their full height. For pure white flowers grow 'White Pearl' ♥, for pink flowers, 'Rosa Perle' ♥.

H: 2m (6ft)

❄❄❄ ◊ ☼ ◐ ♥

Lathyrus odoratus

This sweet pea is an annual climber that uses its tendrils to climb nearby supports. There are many named varieties producing flowers in a wide range of colours, including bicolours. Many are grown for cutting, especially those noted for their heady fragrance.

H: up to 2m (6ft)

❄❄❄ ◊ ☼ ◑

Lonicera x heckrottii

A twining honeysuckle that is semi-evergreen in mild areas but otherwise deciduous. In summer, it produces fragrant flowers that are pink on the outside with orange-yellow throats. Provide a sturdy support to take the weight of mature specimens.

H: 5m (15ft)

❄❄❄ ◑ ◊ ☼ ◑

Lonicera periclymenum 'Graham Thomas'

This venerable honeysuckle flowers all summer. Its fragrant white blooms turn yellow as they age, giving the display a two-tone effect. Grow on a pergola or through an old tree. Prune stems after flowering.

H: 7m (22ft)

❄❄❄ ◊ ○ ☼ ☀ ♈

Lonicera periclymenum 'Serotina'

One of the most fragrant of climbing plants, this honeysuckle grows vigorously through shrubs and trees or over arches and pergolas. It has lush foliage in spring and purple-streaked white flowers in mid- to late summer. Its scent is strongest in the evening.

H: 7m (22ft)

❄❄❄ ◊ ☼ ☀ ♈

Lophospermum erubescens

An evergreen climber with triangular, mid-green leaves and rose-pink tubular flowers borne throughout summer and autumn. Inside the throat of each bloom, the pink colour graduates to white with pink speckles. In cold areas, grow in a greenhouse.

H: 3m (10ft)

❄ ◊ ○ ☼ ☀ ♈

Maurandella antirrhiniflora

The perennial snapdragon is generally grown as an annual. Dotted between the lush green leaves in summer are tubular flowers in shades of purple, violet, or pink, with white throats. Can be grown all year round in a greenhouse.

H: 1–2m (3–6ft)

❄ ◊ ○ ☼ ☀

Mutisia

These evergreen shrubs with daisy-like flowers climb by means of leaf tendrils. *M. oligodon* has toothed, glossy green leaves and pink flowers from summer to autumn. *M. decurrens* has bright orange blooms. They need a sheltered spot.

H: up to 3m (10ft)

❄❄ ◊ ○ ☼ ☀

Parthenocissus henryana

This elegant, vigorous, deciduous climber has green, palmate leaves marked with white veins. In autumn, it puts on a fiery display when its leaves turn crimson before falling. It climbs using disk-like suckers and is perfect for covering unsightly walls.

H: 10m (30ft)

❄❄❄ ◊ ○ ☼ ☀ ♈

Climbers (Pa–St)

Parthenocissus quinquefolia
The Virginia creeper's mid-green foliage provides an attractive screen in summer but this plant really comes into its own in autumn when the leaves turn a brilliant red. A vigorous plant, it will scramble up walls and fences or through shrubs and trees.

H: 15m (50ft)
✳✳✳ ⬤ ☼ ♈ ♆

Parthenocissus tricuspidata
The Boston ivy makes an eye-catching sight on a high wall or building. It is a vigorous climber, quickly clothing its support. The mid-green leaves take on a vivid red-purple hue in autumn before falling. Prune wayward stems to keep the plant within bounds.

H: 20m (70ft)
✳✳✳ ⬤ ☼ ♆

Passiflora caerulea
The exotic-looking blue passion flower brings pergolas, trellis, and arches to life when its white and blue-purple flowers open in summer. Mature plants may produce inedible orange fruits in autumn. 'Constance Elliott' is a pure white form.

H: 10m (30ft)
✳✳ ◗ ⬤ ☼ ♆

Pileostegia viburnoides
A woody, evergreen climber with dark green leathery leaves, this climber carries creamy-white, star-like flowers in dense flowerheads in late summer and autumn. These are held out and away from the foliage, giving a welcome display of colour.

H: 6m (20ft)
✳✳ ◗ ☼ ☼ ♆

Rhodochiton atrosanguineus
The flowers of this perennial climber look like miniature pink parachutes with narrow purple tubes suspended beneath them. The heart-shaped, mid-green leaves are also attractive. The plant is often grown as an annual in frost-prone areas.

H: 3m (10ft)
✳ ◗ ⬤ ☼ ♆

Schisandra
The most commonly grown example of this plant is *Schisandra rubriflora*, which, from late spring to summer, produces bright red flowers on long stalks. It has rounded leaves and twining, woody stems. Female plants produce red fruits.

H: 10m (30ft)
✳✳✳ ◗ ⬤ ☼ ☼

Schizophragma integrifolium

Resembling the climbing hydrangea but with slightly larger leaves and flowerheads, this plant has finely toothed, dark green foliage and floaty white flowers in midsummer. Prune after flowering if necessary to control vigorous stems.

H: 12m (40ft)

❀❀ ◐ ☀ ☼ ☀ ♈

Smilax

These scrambling climbers have slightly spiny stems and glossy green leaves. *S. aspera* bears small fragrant flowers in late summer; *S. china* flowers in late spring. Grow in a conservatory or outdoors in summer in a sheltered site.

H: up to 5m (15ft)

❀❀ ◐ ◐ ☀ ☼

Solanum crispum

This scrambling evergreen or semi-evergreen shrub is a valuable addition to the garden. *S. crispum* 'Glasnevin' ♈ has slender, mid-green leaves and sprays of long-lasting, blue-purple flowers in summer. Prune as necessary after flowering.

H: 6m (20ft)

❀❀ ◐ ◐ ☀ ☼ ♈

Solanum laxum

This vigorous evergreen or semi-evergreen scrambling climber has glossy green foliage and fragrant blue flowers in summer and autumn. *S. laxum* 'Album' ♈ has white flowers with a yellow eye. Grow in a greenhouse in frost-prone areas.

H: 6m (20ft)

❀ ◐ ◐ ☀

Sollya heterophylla

A twining, evergreen Australian native grown for its bell-shaped, blue flowers produced from early summer to autumn. It can be grown in a container up a wigwam or obelisk. Bring indoors in cold areas in winter.

H: 1.5–2m (5–6ft)

❀ ◐ ◐ ☀ ☼ ♈

Stauntonia hexaphylla

A fast-growing, evergreen climber with hanging mauve-tinged, cup-shaped flowers borne in small clusters in spring. It is a useful screen for an unsightly wall or view. Female plants produce purple fruit in autumn. Prune after flowering or in early spring.

H: 10m (30ft)

❀❀ ◐ ☀ ☼

Climbers (Te–Wi)

Tecoma capensis

An evergreen shrub best grown against a very sunny wall or, in colder areas, in a container that can be brought inside during winter. Tubular orange flowers are produced in summer. *T. capensis* 'Aurea' (pictured) has golden yellow flowers.

H: 2–7m (6–22ft)

❄ ◑ ◊ ☼ ♛

Thunbergia alata

Black-eyed Susan is a very decorative evergreen perennial. It is most often grown as an annual for its profusion of bright orange-yellow blooms with distinctive black eyes. It is a good candidate for a large pot, trained up a metal or wooden pyramid.

H: 2.5m (8ft)

❄ ◑ ◊ ☼

Trachelospermum asiaticum

This woody evergreen climber has glossy green foliage and small fragrant white flowers that fade to yellow. It makes a fine climbing wall shrub if trained along wires or trellis, and will create a centrepiece in a container with a pyramid for support.

H: 6m (20ft)

❄❄ ◊ ☼ ♛

Trachelospermum jasminoides

With its profusion of distinctive, propeller-like, fragrant white flowers in summer, the star jasmine is a first-rate climbing plant. Its twining, woody stems soon become clothed in glossy, dark-green leaves that take on a bronze hue in winter.

H: 9m (28ft)

❄❄ ◊ ☼ ♛

Tropaeolum majus

There is a variety of climbing forms of the annual nasturtium, popular for long-lasting displays of summer blooms in colours from creamy-white to deep red. They may be single or double-flowered; some forms offer variegated foliage.

H: 1–3m (3–10ft)

❄ ◑ ◊ ☼

Tropaeolum peregrinum

Attractive for both its blue-green leaves and canary-yellow flowers, this vigorous climber, grown as an annual, will enliven pergolas and pyramids. Feathery, almost wing-like flowers appear from summer to autumn.

H: 2.5–4m (8–12ft)

❀ ◊ ☼

Tropaeolum speciosum
The flame creeper, so-called because of its fiery red flowers, is a dramatic addition to the garden. In summer until autumn, the vivid red, spurred blooms of this perennial appear along the stems. The flowers seek sun, but the roots prefer shade.

H: 3m (10ft) or more
❄❄ ◐ ○ ☼ ☼ ♈

Tropaeolum tuberosum
This is a tuberous-rooted perennial with greyish-green leaves and small orange and yellow flowers that are suspended above the foliage on long stalks. These open from mid-summer through to autumn. In very cold areas, lift and store the tubers over winter.

H: 2–4m (6–12ft)
❄ ◐ ○ ☼

Tweedia caerulea
A shrubby evergreen with unusual flower colour. Hairy stems give rise to downy, light green leaves. From summer until early autumn, it produces turquoise-blue, star-like flowers. Bring indoors in winter in frost-prone areas.

H: 60–100cm (24–39in)
❀❄ ◐ ○ ☼ ♈

Vitis coignetiae
This magnificent, vigorous, deciduous climber has broad, plate-like leaves with crinkled surfaces and felty undersides. It is a vision in autumn, when the leaves turn bright red and purple. Provide a strong pergola or robust wall trellis to take its weight.

H: 15m (50ft)
❄❄❄ ○ ☼ ☼ ♈

Wisteria floribunda 'Multijuga'
A striking climber, wisteria produces hanging flower stems of fragrant lilac-blue blooms, up to 1.2m (4ft) long. These long-lived plants become heavy with age, so need strong support. Prune regularly to ensure an annual flowering spectacle.

H: 9m (28ft) or more
❄❄❄ ◐ ○ ☼ ☼ ♈

Wisteria x formosa
A vigorous, twining, woody climber with a graceful appearance. In late spring and early summer, mauve-purple, pea-like flowers are produced, adding fragrance as well as colour to the display. Furry, runner bean-like seed pods often form after flowering.

H: 9m (28ft)
❄❄❄ ◐ ○ ☼ ☼

Roses (Al–Go)

Rosa '*Albertine*'
A fast-growing, reliable rambler that flowers once, profusely, in midsummer. The double to fully double blooms are light salmon-pink with a strong scent. Train stems along a low wall or fence for a low-level floral display. Prune in summer, after flowering.

H: to 5m (15ft)
❄❄❄ ◗ ◌ ☼ ♈

Rosa '*Aloha*'
A short climber with leathery, dark green leaves and an abundance of fully double pink flowers from summer to autumn. Prune to keep the main shoots within bounds and cut back side shoots by two-thirds between late autumn and early spring.

H: to 3m (12ft)
❄❄❄ ◗ ◌ ☼ ♈

Rosa banksiae '*Lutea*'
A charming climbing rose with thornless stems and clusters of many fully double, straw-yellow, lightly scented flowers in late spring. For the best displays, plant in a sheltered position. Prune flowering stems between late autumn and early spring.

H: to 6m (20ft)
❄❄ ◗ ◌ ☼ ♈

Rosa '*Bobbie James*'
This very vigorous rambler produces huge heads of creamy-white, semi-double flowers in summer. The glossy leaves open reddish-green, turning mid-green with age. It is perfect for covering a large outbuilding. Prune in summer, after flowering.

H: to 10m (30ft)
❄❄❄ ◗ ◌ ☼ ♈

Rosa *Breath of Life*
A climbing hybrid tea rose producing apricot-pink, rounded, fully double, fragrant flowers in flushes, from summer until autumn. Train it to wires against a wall or over an arch where its blooms can be appreciated. Prune between late autumn and early spring.

H: 2.5m (8ft)
❄❄❄ ◗ ◌ ☼

Rosa '*Climbing Iceberg*'
This free-flowering rose is a striking sight when covered with pure white double flowers from summer until autumn, especially when allowed to reach its full height, such as against a house wall. Prune between late autumn and early spring.

H: 3m (10ft)
❄❄❄ ◗ ◌ ☼ ♈

Rosa 'Climbing Mrs Sam McGredy'

This is a very vigorous climbing hybrid tea rose with copper-red leaves and large, copper-red to salmon-pink flowers, produced mainly in summer. It can be grown through trees and is tolerant of poorer soils. Prune between late autumn and early spring.

H: 3m (10ft)
✽✽✽ ◐ ◊ ☼ ♉

Rosa 'Compassion'

An upright, climbing hybrid tea rose producing from summer to autumn fragrant, double, salmon-pink flowers tinted with apricot. The glossy dark green leaves are generally disease-free. Prune between late autumn and early spring.

H: 3m (10ft)
✽✽✽ ◐ ◊ ☼ ♉

Rosa Dublin Bay

A repeat-flowering, climbing floribunda that produces large clusters of double red flowers from summer to autumn. It can be grown as a climber against a wall or an arch, or pruned to form a shrub. Prune from late autumn to early spring.

H: 2.2m (7ft)
✽✽✽ ◐ ◊ ☼ ♉

Rosa 'Félicité Perpétue'

A reliable, semi-evergreen rambler that in summer produces rosette-shaped, fully double, creamy-white blooms from pink-tinted buds. It is a strong grower, making a dense mass of foliage and flowers. Prune in summer, after flowering.

H: to 5m (15ft)
✽✽✽ ◐ ◊ ☼ ♉

Rosa 'François Juranville'

A rambler with glossy foliage and long, graceful stems. In summer, it bears clusters of rosette-shaped, fully double, salmon-pink flowers that turn yellow towards their bases and fill the air with the scent of apples. Prune in summer, after flowering.

H: 6m (20ft)
✽✽✽ ◐ ◊ ☼ ♉

Rosa 'Golden Showers'

An upright climbing rose with a long flowering season that is ideal for shadier situations. It bears large, fragrant, double to semi-double, golden-yellow blooms that fade to cream. Prune between late autumn and early spring.

H: to 3m (10ft)
✽✽✽ ◐ ◊ ☼ ♉

Roses (Ha–Ze)

Rosa *Handel*

An upright, sturdy climbing rose with glossy dark green leaves and attractive double flowers that are pale pink edged with darker pink. It flowers from summer right through until winter. Prune between late autumn and early spring.

H: 3m (10ft)

✿✿✿ ◗ ◗ ☼ ♔

Rosa *Laura Ford*

From summer until autumn, this upright, miniature climbing rose produces clusters of lightly scented, semi-double, yellow blooms. As the flowers fade, their edges become tinged with pink. Prune between late autumn and early spring.

H: 2.2m (7ft)

✿✿✿ ◗ ◗ ☼ ♔

Rosa *'New Dawn'*

A vigorous climber with arching stems, glossy foliage and clusters of pale-pink, cupped, double flowers with a fresh fragrance from summer until autumn. This rose tolerates poorer soils and shadier sites. Prune between late autumn and early spring.

H: 3m (10ft)

✿✿✿ ◗ ◗ ☼ ♔

Rosa *'Phyllis Bide'*

Unlike most rambling roses, this one repeat flowers from summer until autumn, producing sprays of fragrant, yellow blooms with pink-flushed petals. Leaves are mid-green with narrow leaflets. Prune in summer, after flowering.

H: 2.5m (8ft)

✿✿✿ ◗ ◗ ☼ ♔

Rosa *'Pink Perpétué'*

This versatile, repeat-flowering climbing rose has dark green foliage and fully double, slightly scented, rose-pink blooms that are darker on the reverse. It flowers from summer until autumn. Prune between late autumn and early spring.

H: to 3m (10ft)

✿✿✿ ◗ ◗ ☼

Rosa *'Sander's White Rambler'*

A strong-growing rambling rose with shiny pale green foliage and sprays of small, scented, white, double flowers carried on lax stems in late summer. It tolerates shady sites and poorer soils and is vigorous enough to train into trees. Prune in summer after flowering.

H: 4m (12ft)

✿✿✿ ◗ ◗ ☼ ♔

Rosa *'Schoolgirl'*
This hybrid tea climbing rose is a repeat-flowering variety producing large, double, deep apricot flowers. The scented blooms are carried from summer until autumn. The dark green foliage is rather sparse. Prune between late autumn and early spring.

H: 3m (10ft)
❄❄❄ ◐ ◊ ☀

Rosa *'Seagull'*
This vigorous rambler has arching stems, grey-green foliage, and a profusion of small, creamy-white, single to semi-double flowers with a cluster of yellow stamens at the centre. It flowers throughout summer. Prune in summer, after flowering.

H: 6m (20ft)
❄❄❄ ◐ ◊ ☀ ♀

Rosa *Summer Wine*
A beautiful, repeat-flowering, vigorous, climbing rose with single, coral-pink, fragrant flowers from summer to autumn. The yellow centre of each flower has a cluster of red anthers. Prune between late autumn and early spring.

H: 3m (10ft)
❄❄❄ ◐ ◊ ☀ ♀

Rosa *Warm Welcome*
This miniature climber is one of the most free-flowering of all climbing roses. Its double, orange-red flowers cover the entire plant from summer to autumn. It is ideal for pillars and beside doorways. Prune between late autumn and early spring.

H: 2.2m (7ft)
❄❄❄ ◐ ◊ ☀ ♀

Rosa *'Wedding Day'*
A strong-growing rambling rose that in summer produces large clusters of highly scented, creamy-yellow, single flowers that are tinged apricot in bud and later turn white. Grow up into a tree or train onto a large pergola. Prune in summer, after flowering.

H: 8m (25ft)
❄❄❄ ◐ ◊ ☀

Rosa *'Zéphirine Drouhin'*
Known for its thornless stems, this bourbon climbing rose has an open, lax habit and many very fragrant, deep pink, double flowers from summer to autumn. It will grow on a shady wall and makes a fine hedge. Prune between late autumn and early spring.

H: 3m (10ft)
❄❄❄ ◐ ◊ ☀

Suppliers

Clematis

Beeches Nursery
Village Centre
Ashdon
Saffron Walden
Essex CB10 2HB
Tel: 01799 584362
www.beechesnursery.co.uk

Burford Garden Company
Burford House Gardens
Tenbury Wells
Worcestershire WR15 8HQ
Tel: 01584 810777
Email: info@burford.co.uk
www.burford.co.uk

Guernsey Clematis Nursery
Domarie Vineries
Les Sauvagees
St Sampsons
Guernsey GY2 4FD
Tel: 01481 245942
Email: raymondjevison@guernsey-
   clematis.com
www.guernsey-clematis.com

Sheila Chapman Clematis
Coveney Nursery
160 Ongar Road
Abridge
Essex RM4 1AA
Tel: 01708 688090
Email: sheilachapman@hotmail.co.uk
www.sheilachapman.co.uk

Sherston Parva Nursery
Malmesbury Road
Sherston
Wiltshire SN16 0NX
Tel: 01666 840348
Email: sherstonparva@aol.com
www.sherstonparva.com

Taylors Clematis Nursery
Sutton
Askern
Doncaster
South Yorkshire DN6 9JZ
Tel: 01302 708415
Email: info@taylorsclematis.co.uk
www.taylorsclematis.co.uk

Thorncroft Clematis Nursery
Reymerston
Norwich
Norfolk NR9 4QG
Tel: 01953 850407
Email: sales@thorncroft.co.uk
www.thorncroft.co.uk

Climbers

J Bradshaw & Son
Busheyfield Nursery
Herne
Herne Bay
Kent CT6 7JL
Tel: 01227 375415

Burncoose Nurseries
Gwennap
Redruth
Cornwall TR16 6BJ
Tel: 01209 860316
Email: info@burncoose.co.uk
www.burncoose.co.uk

Crûg Farm Plants
Griffith's Crossing
Caernarfon
Gwynedd LL55 1TU
Tel: 01248 670232
Email: info@crug-farm.co.uk
www.crug-farm.co.uk

Eagle Sweet Peas
Broadmoor Lane
Stowe-by-Chartley
Staffordshire ST18 0LD
Tel: 01889 270215
Email: sales@eaglesweetpeas.co.uk
www.eaglesweetpeas.co.uk

Fibrex Nurseries
Honeybourne Road
Pebworth
Stratford-upon-Avon
Warwickshire CV37 8XP
Tel: 01789 720788
Email: sales@fibrex.co.uk
www.fibrex.co.uk

Goscote Nurseries Ltd
Syston Road
Cossington
Leicestershire LE7 4UZ
Tel: 01509 812121
Email: sales@goscote.co.uk
www.goscote.co.uk

Hillier Nurseries
The Stables
Ampfield House
Ampfield
Romsey
Hampshire SO51 9BQ
Tel: 01794 368733
Email: andrewmcindoe@hillier.co.uk
www.hillier.co.uk

Hopleys Plants
High Street
Much Hadham
Hertfordshire SG10 6BU
Tel: 01279 842509
Email: sales@hopleys.co.uk
www.hopleys.co.uk

Matthewman's Sweetpeas
14 Chariot Way
Thorpe Audlin
Pontefract
West Yorks WF8 3EZ
Tel: 01977 621381
Email: sales@sweetpeasonline.co.uk
www.sweetpeasonline.co.uk

Roseland House Nursery
Chacewater
Truro
Cornwall TR4 8QB
Tel: 01872 560451
clematis@roselandhouse.co.uk
www.roselandhouse.co.uk

Squires Garden Centre
Sixth Cross Road
Twickenham
Middlesex TW2 5PA
Tel: 020 8977 9988
Email: sarah@squiresgardencentre.
   co.uk
www.squiresgardencentres.co.uk

**Stone House Cottage Garden &
Nursery**
Stone
Near Kidderminster
Worcestershire DY10 4BG
Tel: 01562 69902
Email: louisa@shcn.co.uk
www.shcn.co.uk

Thompson & Morgan
Poplar Lane
Ipswich
Suffolk IP8 3BU
Tel: 01473 695200
www.thompson-morgan.com

Trevena Cross Nurseries
Breage
Helston
Cornwall TR13 9PS
Tel: 01736 763880
Email: info@trevenacross.co.uk
www.trevenacross.co.uk

Roses

Crocus.co.uk
Nursery Court
London Road
Windlesham
Surrey GU20 6LQ
Tel: 0870 787 1414
www.crocus.co.uk

David Austin Roses
Bowling Green Lane
Albrighton
Wolverhampton WV7 3HB
Tel: 01902 376300
Email: retail@davidaustinroses.com
www.davidaustinroses.com

Harkness Roses
The Rose Garden
Cambridge Road
Hitchin
Hertfordshire SG4 0JT
Tel: 01462 420402 / 0845 331 3143
Email: harkness@roses.co.uk
www.roses.co.uk

Peter Beales Roses
London Road
Attleborough
Norfolk NR17 1AY
Tel: 01953 454707
Email: sales@peterbealesroses.co.uk
www.classicroses.co.uk

Pococks Roses
Jermyns Lane
Romsey
Hampshire SO51 0QA
Tel: 01794 367500
Email: sales@pococksroses.co.uk
www.pococksroses.co.uk

Robert Mattock Roses
The Rose Nurseries
Lodge Hill
Abingdon
Oxford OX14 2JD
Tel: 01865 735382
Email: robert@robertmattockroses
   .com
www.robertmattockroses.com

Scented Roses
Little Silver House
Romansleigh
South Molton
Devon
Tel: 01769 550485

Wych Cross Nurseries
Wych Cross
Forest Row
East Grinstead
West Sussex RH18 5JW
Tel: 01342 822705
Email: roses@wychcross.co.uk
www.wychcross.co.uk

Climbing supports

Forest Garden plc
Tel: 0870 191 9800
Email: info@forestgarden.co.uk
www.forestgarden.co.uk

Index

Index

Acknowledgements

The publisher would like to thank the following for their kind permission to reproduce their photographs:

(Key: a-above; b-below/bottom; c-centre; l-left; r-right; t-top)

6-7: DK Images: Steve Wooster/RHS Chelsea Flower Show 2001/Brighstone and District Horticultural Society. **8:** Leigh Clapp: (t). Andrew Lawson: Barnsley House, Glos. (b). **9:** Andrew Lawson. **10:** S & O Mathews Photography: The Little Cottage, Lymington, Hants (l), The Garden Collection: Liz Eddison/ Hampton Court Flower Show 2000/ Designer: Paul Stone (r). **11:** Marianne Majerus Photography: Coughton Court, Warks (l). **12:** The Garden Collection: Gary Rogers/Designers: Ngaere Mackay & David Seeler (bl). John Glover: Bransford Nursery, Worcs. (t). **13:** Marianne Majerus Photography: RHS Rosemoor. **14:** Andrew Lawson: Pine House, Leics. (tl), The Garden Collection: Liz Eddison (tr) (b); Liz Eddison/Designer: Bob Purnell (tc). **15:** Andrew Lawson: RHS Chelsea 1996/ Designer Stephen Woodhams. **17:** The Garden Collection: Jonathan Buckley/ Designer: Christopher Lloyd, Great Dixter (tl), S & O Mathews Photography: Pashley Manor, Sussex (tr), Modeste Herwig: Theetuin, Weesp, The Netherlands (b). **18:** John Glover: Kew Gardens, Surrey. **19:** Modeste Herwig: Manor House, Birlingham (t), The Garden Collection: Liz Eddison (b). **20:** The Garden Collection: Liz Eddison/Chelsea Flower Show 2004/ Designer: Stephen Hall (t); Liz Eddison/ RHS Chelsea Flower Show 2003/Designer: Kay Yamada (br). Andrew Lawson: (bl).

21: Derek St Romaine. **22:** Marianne Majerus Photography: Knoll House. **23:** The Garden Collection: Liz Eddison (t). Andrew Lawson: (b). **24:** The Garden Collection: Liz Eddison (t), DK Images: Steve Wooster/ RHS Chelsea Flower Show 2001/Brighstone Horticultural Club (bl), John Glover: (br). **26:** Derek St Romaine: RHS Rosemoor (t), Marianne Majerus Photography: Bedfield Hall, Suffolk (b). **27:** Derek St Romaine: Mr and Mrs Lusby (t), Marianne Majerus Photography: Designer: Kevin Wilson (bl), DK Images: Steve Wooster/RHS Chelsea Flower Show 2001/Heathend Garden Club (br). **28:** S & O Mathews Photography: North Court, Isle of Wight (t), John Glover: (b). **29:** Leigh Clapp: Houghton Lodge (r). Derek St Romaine: Mr and Mrs Borrett (bl). **30:** The Garden Collection: Derek Harris (t). S & O Mathews Photography: Eastern Cottage, Yarmouth, IOW (b). **31:** S & O Mathews Photography: (t), The Garden Collection: Gary Rogers/ Designers: Ngaere Mackay & David Seeler (b). **32:** Andrew Lawson: (t) (b). **33:** Derek St Romaine. **36:** John Glover: (t). **38:** The Garden Collection: Liz Eddison/Designer: Bob Purnell (t). **39:** Leigh Clapp: (t). **64–65:** Modeste Herwig: Gardens of the Rose. **66:** The Guernsey Clematis Nursery Ltd/Thompson & Morgan. **69:** Nicola Stocken Tomkins: Gantsmill, Bruton, Somerset. **70:** S & O Mathews Photography: (bl). **71:** S & O Mathews Photography. **72:** Garden World Images: (tr). **73:** Andrew Lawson: Cothay Manor, Somerset. **74:** Clive Nichols: Lower House Farm, Gwent (bl). **75:** Clive Nichols: Lower House Farm, Gwent. **77:** Harpur Garden Library: Marcus Harpus/Mr & Mrs

Grice, Essex. **79:** Leigh Clapp: Hannath Garden. **81:** John Glover: RHS Chelsea Flower Show 1991/Agriframes. **83:** Andrew Lawson. **85:** DK Images: Mark Winwood/Hampton Court Flower Show 2005/Elysium Design by Paul Hensey. **86:** The Garden Collection: Jonathan Buckley/Designer: Christopher Lloyd (tl). **87:** The Garden Collection: Jonathan Buckley/Designer: Christopher Lloyd. **96:** Leigh Clapp: Meadow Cottage (t). **98:** Mark Winwood: (tr) (br). **99:** Mark Winwood. **116:** Holt Studios International: Michael Mayer/FLPA (tr). **117:** RHS Tim Sandall (c), (cr). **118:** RHS Tim Sandall (bl). **119:** Modeste Herwig: (tl), RHS Tim Sandall (tr). **140:** Garden World Images: (bl). **141:** Garden World Images: (tl). **142:** Garden World Images: (bc). **145:** Thompson & Morgan (bl). **146:** Garden Picture Library: J S Sira (br). **150:** crocus.co.uk (tl). **153:** crocus. co.uk (bc).

All other images © Dorling Kindersley For further information see: www.dkimages.com

Dorling Kindersley would also like to thank the following:
Editors for Airedale Publishing: Helen Ridge, Fiona Wild, Mandy Lebentz *Designers for Airedale Publishing*: Elly King, Murdo Culver *Index*: Michèle Clarke

Forest Garden (www.forestgarden.co.uk) for supplying the rose arch and border edging on pp.44–5.